OCCASIONAL PUBLICATION No. 15

SUPPLEMENTS TO DODSLEY'S COLLECTION OF POEMS

by

Harold Forster

Oxford Bibliographical Society
Bodleian Library
Oxford
1980

Produced by Comersgate Limited, St. Clements, Oxford

CONTENTS

ABBREVIATIONS

A. *Supplements*
   F63: Fawkes, *The Poetical Calendar*, 12 vols, 1763. (Collations, 1a)
   M67: Mendez, *Collection of the most esteemed Pieces of Poetry*, 1767. (2a)
   M70: ———, 2nd edition, 1770. (2b)
   P68a: Pearch, *Collection of Poems*, 2 vols, 1768, 1st issue. (3a(i))
   P68b: ———, 2nd issue. (3a(ii))
   P70: ———, 4 vols, 1770. (3b)
   P75: ———, 4 vols, revised, 1775. (3c)
   P83: ———, 4 vols, new edition with biographical notes by Isaac Reed, 1783.
      (3d)

B. *References*
   Al.Cantab.: Alumni Cantabrigienses, ed. J. Venn, 10 vols, 1922-54.
   Al.Dublin.: Alumni Dublinienses, ed. G. Burnell & T. Sadleir, 1935.
   Al.Oxon.: Alumni Oxonienses, 1715-1886, ed. J. Foster, 4 vols, 1887-8.
   Ault: *Alexander Pope. Minor Poems.* ed. N. Ault & G. Butt, 1964.
   Biog.Dram: Biographia Dramatica, ed. Stephen Jones, 3 vols, 1812.
   Brooks: *The Percy Letters*, ed. Cleanth Brooks *et al.* (*Hailes*: Correspondence with David Dalrymple, Lord Hailes, 1954; *Shenstone*, — with William Shenstone, 1977).
   Chalmers: *The Works of the English Poets*, ed. Alexander Chalmers, 21 vols, 1812.
   Courtney: *Dodsley's Collection of Poetry. Its Contents and Contributors.* By W.P. Courtney. Privately printed, London, 1910.
   CR: The Critical Review, 70 vols, 1756-90.
   DNB: The Dictionary of National Biography, 22 vols, repr., 1968.
   Foxon: *English Verse, 1701-1750.* By D. Foxon. 2 vols, 1975.
   GM: The Gentleman's Magazine, 1731-1868.
   Halkett & Laing: *Dictionary of Anonymous and Pseudonymous English Literature*, ed. S. Halkett & J. Laing, revised, 7 vols, 1926-34.
   Hill: *The Letters of Samuel Johnson*, ed. G. Birkbeck Hill, 2 vols, 1892.
   Hoare: *The History of Modern Wiltshire*, by Sir R.C. Hoare, 1822-34. (Hundreds of *Ambresbury; Downton; Dunworth*).
   Lewis: *Horace Walpole's Correspondence*, ed. W.S. Lewis, 49 vols, 1937-date. (*Berry*, Correspondence with Mary Berry, 2 vols, 1944; *Cole*, — with Rev. William Cole, 2 vols, 1937; *Deffand*, — with Mme. du Deffand, 6 vols, 1939; *Mann*, — with Sir Horace Mann, 11 vols, 1955-71).
   Little & Kahrl: *The Letters of David Garrick*, ed. D.M. Little & G.M. Kahrl, 3 vols, 1963.
   L. Stage: The London Stage, 1660-1800. Part 4 (1747-1776), ed. G.W. Stone, 1962.
   Manning & Bray: *The History and Antiquities of Surrey*, by O. Manning & W. Bray, 3 vols, 1804-14.
   Mid.Temple: The Register of Admissions to the Middle Temple, ed. H.A.C. Sturgess, 3 vols, 1949.
   MR: The Monthly Review, 1st series, 81 vols, 1749-89.

New CBEL: The New Cambridge Bibliography of English Literature, Vol.2, 1660-1800, ed. G. Watson, 1971.

NFH: The New Foundling Hospital for Wit, new edition, 6 vols, 1784.

Nichol Smith: *The Poems of Samuel Johnson*, ed. D. Nichol Smith & E.L. McAdam, 2nd edition, 1974.

Nichols, *Illust.: Illustrations of the Literary History of the Eighteenth Century*, by John Nichols, 8 vols, 1817-58.

N&Q: Notes & Queries, 1849-date.

Old Westminsters: The Record of Old Westminsters, ed. G.F. Russell Barker & A.H. Stenning, 2 vols, 1928.

Reliques: The Reliques of Ancient English Poetry, ed. T. Percy, 3 vols, 5th edition, 1812.

Williams: *The Letters of William Shenstone*, ed. Marjorie Williams, 1939.

INTRODUCTION

In 1933 Dr. R.W. Chapman published in the *Proceedings of the Oxford Biblio-graphical Society*, vol.III, part iii, a paper on Dodsley's *Collection of Poems by Several Hands*, giving collations, lists and indices of all the editions up to the completion of the miscellany in 1758. My intention is to extend the work of Chapman by dealing in the same way with the professed "Supplements to Dodsley", so that it will be in effect a "Supplement to Chapman".

The collections in question are three: *The Poetical Calendar*, 12 volumes, 1763, which announced on its title-page that it was "intended as a Supplement to Mr. Dodsley's Collection"; *A Collection of the most esteemed Pieces of Poetry*, Richardson and Urquhart, 1 volume, 1767 (second edition 1770), "by the late Moses Mendez, Esq; and other Contributors to Dodsley's Collection. To which this is intended as a Supplement"; and *A Collection of Poems . . . by Several Hands*, printed for G. Pearch, 2 volumes, 1768; 4 volumes 1770 (new editions: 1775, 1783), which the editor in his Advertisement hoped "will not be considered as an improper Supplement to the work of which they are designed as a Continuation".

The eight volumes of Nichols's *Select Collection of Poems*, 1780-1784, fall into a rather different category and have therefore not been included here. Nichols's aim was not so much to produce an anthology of the latest verse as to conduct a poetical mopping-up operation and he claimed the collection not as a "supplement" but as a "suitable appendage" to Dodsley, Pearch and the sixty volumes of the English Poets. He admitted in his Advertisement that the collection was "formed principally from that of Mr. Dryden", filled out by those of Fenton and Steele, with selections from the miscellanies of Pope, Pemberton, Lintot and Tooke — all pre-Dodsley material. Actually, some of the later volumes, particularly VI and VIII, contain a fair proportion of post-Dodsley poetry, including some pieces by Nichols himself. But the bulk of the collection consists of Restoration and Augustan verse, which makes it unsuitable for inclusion as a "Supplement to Dodsley".

Bell's *Classical Arrangement of Fugitive Poetry*, 16 volumes, 1789-1794, was not an original miscellany but a rehash of the material from other collections, particularly the "Supplements"; while such series as *The Foundling Hospital for Wit*, 6 volumes, 1743-1749, *The New Foundling Hospital*, 6 volumes, 1768-1773, *The Fugitive Miscellany*, 2 volumes 1774-1775, and *The Asylum for Fugitives*, 4 volumes, 1785-1793, consist of politico-satirical verse, following in the footsteps of *Poems on Affairs of State*, whereas Dodsley and the "Supplements" followed the pattern of "Dryden's" *Miscellanies*. The remainder of the enormous list of miscellanies in the *New CBEL* will be found, on examination, to consist largely of song-books and jest-books with a comparatively small number of serious collections of modern poetry. The latter often have some special angle, moral, festive, feminine, Scottish and so on, and in any case, as single volumes, they do not qualify for the "Dodsley" class. It is not unreasonable, therefore, to confine this paper to the *professed* "Supplements to Dodsley".

Of the three, the closest to Dodsley in form and spirit is the third, Pearch's *Collection*. The four volumes can sometimes be found bound uniformly and numbered consecutively with sets of Dodsley. The same is true of the 1767 collection conventionally referred to, for convenience, as "Mendez" rather than "Richardson and Urquhart", but it consists of only a single volume. But *The Poetical Calendar*, edited by Francis Fawkes and William Woty, is so different that one might hesitate to class it as a "Supplement to Dodsley" but for the specific claim of its editors. The twelve volumes, smaller in format and length, were issued month by month over a single year and contained a much larger proportion of "originals", i.e. new poems written by the editors and their friends, notably the introductory odes on the relevant month.

All the editors were careful not to repeat the poems selected by Dodsley — "Mendez" even inserted a note of apology for inadvertently including the old song of *Winifreda*, which had appeared simply as "A Song" in Dodsley, iv,282. But they had no such inhibitions about copying from each other and the popularity of certain poems can be inferred from their appearance in all three anthologies; not only Collins's *Oriental Eclogues*, Johnson's *Winter's Walk*, and Thomas Warton's *Newmarket*, but the pastorals *Autumn* by Thomas Brerewood, and *Day* by John Cunningham, the pseudo-Spenserian *Seasons* of Moses Mendez, and the ubiquitous *Prayer for Indifference* of Mrs. Greville. Of the two hundred or so authors, fifty-three had appeared previously in Dodsley and of these Akenside, Collins, Johnson, Mendez, Thomas Warton and William Whitehead were represented in all three supplements. In the case of Collins the *Poetical Calendar* exceptionally repeated the five poems printed in Dodsley, but only because the editors wished to reprint the whole of the poet's works — the first complete collection of Collins's poetry, anticipating by two years Langhorne's first edition of the *Poetical Works*, 1765.

I have followed the general plan of Chapman — collations, contents, index of authors, index of first lines — with certain modifications and additions, as follows:-

i. *Contents*. Chapman gives the full contents lists for ten volumes, i.e. the original six volumes of Dodsley with the second editions of volumes I-III and the supplementary "Volume IV" of 1749. But with twelve volumes of *The Poetical Calendar*, two of "Mendez" (first and second editions), and sixteen of Pearch (two issues of the first two volumes, with three further editions of four volumes), it is not practicable to print the lists in full for all the volumes. In the later editions, therefore, only the changes — often very considerable — have been noted, i.e. the additions and omissions; minor changes, such as the transference of a poem from one volume to another, have not been listed but the details can be found in the Index of Authors. For these lists the full title of the poem, as printed in the text, has been preferred to the abbreviated version given in the original contents lists, as the latter often omit the author's name and other significant details.

ii. *Authors*. In his Index of Authors, Chapman had not more than two possible references to record for any poem, but here there is a possible maximum of eight. They have therefore been arranged in columns, corresponding to the various editions of the three miscellanies. The two issues of the first edition of Pearch, 1768, are shown in the same column with the variant items marked "a" or "b". This lay-out has the advantage of showing clearly the relative frequency of reprinting of the poems and the numerous revisions of the contents of the collections.

Section A lists the known authors alphabetically; Section B shows those who are identified only by their initials or such phrases as "A Lady" or even "———", where there are a number of poems "By the Same"; Section C is an alphabetical list of the titles of the unidentified anonymous poems.

The attributions of the anonymous poems in Dodsley's *Collection* were taken by Chapman from W.P. Courtney's privately printed *Contents and Contributors to Dodsley's Collection*, 1910, and therefore required no notes. Wherever I have been able to identify the author of an anonymous piece in the "Supplements", I have added a footnote, giving the evidence for the attribution. All the poems printed anonymously (including those identified only by initials, etc.) are marked with an asterisk; but where the author's name is shown in a later edition or another of the miscellanies, no footnote is needed.

iii. *First Lines.* The references against the first lines show the author and the number of the relevant poem in the Index of Authors, where the title will be found.

iv. *Biographical notes.* Courtney included a number of biographical notes on the less-known contributors to Dodsley. I have added a similar section, giving the basic facts of the life and writings of the poets who are *not* to be found in *DNB.*

The collations and lists are based primarily on the copies of the "Supplements" in the British Library, the Bodleian Library, Oxford, and the writer's own collection. The first issue of Pearch's *Collection*, 2 volumes, 1768, is known only in the copies at the Bodleian, and at the Beinecke Library, Yale University. Most sets of the *Poetical Calendar* consist of mixed first and second editions of the twelve volumes, but complete sets of first editions can be found at the British Library, and in the Dyce Collection at the Victoria and Albert Museum.

My thanks are due to the librarians of the above institutions for their ready and helpful response to my enquiries, as also to those of the London Library, Cambridge University, Birmingham University, University College, Cardiff, Trinity College, Dublin, the Folger Library and the Australian National Library, Canberra. I would like to acknowledge particularly the help of Mr. Julian Roberts, Keeper of Printed Books at the Bodleian, in sorting out the problem of the two issues of the first edition of Pearch's *Collection.* (See my note on the subject in the *Bodleian Library Record*, forthcoming).

The title-pages of *The Poetical Calendar*, and of *A Collection of Poems*, are reproduced from copies in the Bodleian Library, Oxford (shelf-marks: 8° K 275 BS.; Godw. subt. 259), by permission of the Curators; that of *A Collection of the Most Esteemed Pieces of Poetry* from a copy in the British Library (press-mark: 11601.dd.18.), by permission of the British Library Board.

1a. *The Poetical Calendar, 1763*

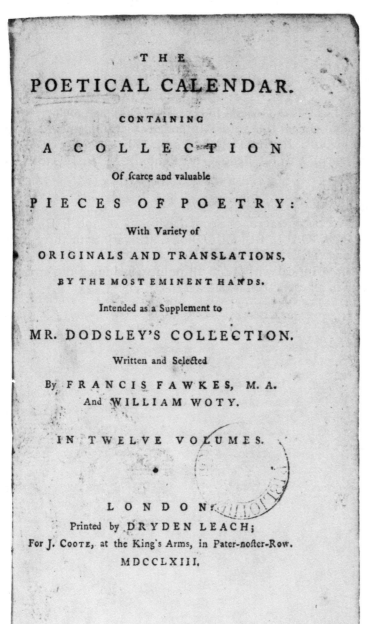

THE

POETICAL CALENDAR.

CONTAINING

A COLLECTION

Of scarce and valuable

PIECES OF POETRY:

With Variety of

ORIGINALS AND TRANSLATIONS,

BY THE MOST EMINENT HANDS.

Intended as a Supplement to

MR. DODSLEY'S COLLECTION.

Written and Selected

By FRANCIS FAWKES, M. A.
And WILLIAM WOTY.

IN TWELVE VOLUMES.

*

LONDON:
Printed by DRYDEN LEACH;
For J. COOTE, at the King's Arms, in Pater-noster-Row.
MDCCLXIII.

Half-titles: The Poetical Calendar. Vol.I. For January. (Vol.II. For February
. . . Vol.XII. For December.)
Sm.8°. Vol.I: A^4 B-H^8 I^4 ; *i-v* vi *vii* viii *1* 2-120. *A*1 hft.
     II: A^2 B-H^8 I^4 K^2 ; *i-iv 1* 2-122 *v* vi. *A*1 hft.
    III: A^2 B-H^8 I^4 K^2 ; *i-iv 1* 2-123 *124*. *A*1 hft.

IV: as III.
V: as III.
VI: A^2 B-H^8 I^4 K^2; *i-iv 1* 2-122 *123* 124. A1 hft.
VII: as III.
VIII: A^2 B-H^8 I^4 K^2; *i-iv 1* 2-122 *123* "123". A1 hft.
IX: as III.
X: as VI.
XI: as VI.
XII: A^2 B-H^8 I^4; *i-iv 1* 2-112 *113-120*. A1 hft.

Advertisement by the editors, Dec.24, 1762, I,*v*-vi; Contents lists, I,*vii*-viii; II,*v*-vi; III-V,*124*; VI,*123*-124; VII,*124*; VIII,*123*-"123"; IX,*124*; X-XI,*123*-124; XII,*113-120*, General Index.

N.B. Only vols.I and II bear the words "Intended as a Supplement . . ." on their title-pages. Catchwords: II,112, TRUTH (for LOVE); VI,111, ODE (for AN); 112, That (for Hence); VIII,60, Bedold (for Behold); XI,79, TO (for THE).

1b.   *The Poetical Calendar, 2nd edition, 1763/4.*
No examples have been traced of second editions of vols.I, II, X, XI, XII. Mixed sets (e.g. at L, O, LL, BU, CU, DFo, ANL) vary with three to seven of vols.III-IX showing THE SECOND EDITION above the imprint. Otherwise they appear to be identical with 1a in all points (including the errors) except for vol.III, which in all cases seen is dated 1764.

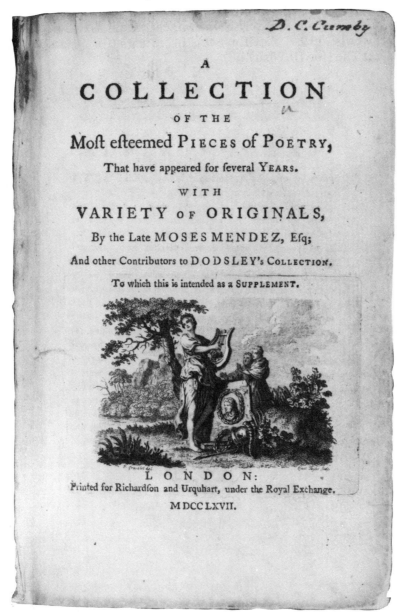

D. C. Cumby

A

COLLECTION

OF THE

Moſt eſteemed PIECES of POETRY,

That have appeared for ſeveral YEARS.

WITH

VARIETY OF ORIGINALS,

By the Late MOSES MENDEZ, Eſq;

And other Contributors to DODSLEY's COLLECTION.

To which this is intended as a SUPPLEMENT.

LONDON:

Printed for Richardſon and Urquhart, under the Royal Exchange.

MDCCLXVII.

8°. A^4 B-X^8 ; *i-viii 1* 2-230.

Advertisement, *iii*; Contents, *v-viii*; with note at end apologising for inadvertent inclusion of song (*Winifreda*) already printed in Dodsley's *Collection*. Engravings at head of text, p.*1*, (moonlit tomb, *Ant.Walker del. Isaac Taylor scu.*) and at end, p.316 (shepherd boy piping, *Bland sculp.*)

N.B. Catchwords: 4, De- (for Is); 41, ON (for TO); 54, A (for EDWIN); 222, XIII (for XII); 276, III (for But); 285, The (for III, What).

Title-page as in 2a, with addition of THE SECOND EDITION above the engraving and the date changed to MDCCLXX.

8°. a^2 b^2 A-T^8 U^6 ; *i-viii 1 2*-316.

Advertisement, *iii*; Contents (revised), *v-viii*; engravings as in 2a.

N.B. Catchwords: 119, I see (for See); 147, Heats (for Hearts); 169, To (for An); 196, III The (for III What).

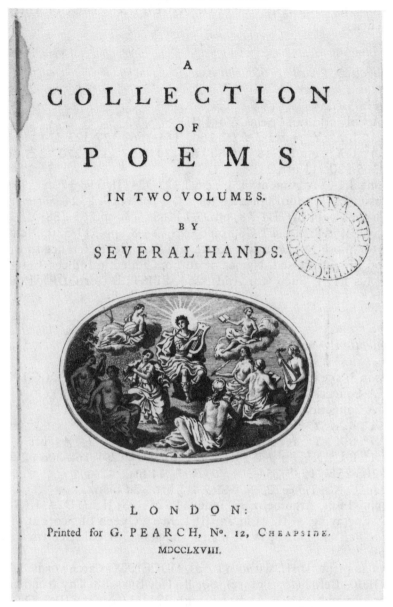

A

COLLECTION

OF

POEMS

IN TWO VOLUMES.

BY

SEVERAL HANDS.

LONDON:

Printed for G. PEARCH, Nº. 12, CHEAPSIDE.

MDCCLXVIII.

Half-titles: A Collection of Poems, being two additional volumes to Mr. Dodsley's Collection. Vol.I (II).

$8°$. Vol.I: A^4 B-X^8 Y^2; *i-iv* 1-3 *4 1* 2-160 "151-166" 177-323 *324*. *A*1 hft.

II: A^2 B-X^8; *i-iv 1* 2-48 "65-80" 65-174 "157" 176-271 "270-318" *A*1 hft.

Advertisement, I,1-3; Argument (of first poem), 4; Index, I,321-323; II,"317-318"; Errata, II,"318". Engravings at head of text, I,1 (monk on seashore; *Isaac Taylor del. et sculp.*); II,1 (Oriental shepherd; *Isaac Taylor del. et sculp.*) "Books printed for and sold by G. Pearch", I,324.

N.B. Title-page, apart from imprint, mimics Dodsley. Indices do not show authors' names. Catchwords: I,3, ADVER- (for ARGUMENT); 150, WRITTEN (for TWO); 200, E'en (for Ev'n); 204, To (for Tho'); 253, When (for Where); 257, The (for Th'); 305, The (for PROLOGUE); II,29, The (for There); 162, There (for Their).

3a(ii). *Pearch's Collection, 2 vols, 1768 (2nd issue)*

Title-page as in 3a(i).
Half-titles: A Collection of Poems. Vol.I (II).
8°. Vol.I: A^4 B-X^8 Y^2; *i-iv* 1-3 *4 1* 2-160 "151-166" 177-323 *324. A*1 hft.
    II: A^2 B-X^8; *i-iv 1* 2-48 "65-80" 65-174 "157" 176-272 "271-302" 305-320. *A*1 hft.
Advertisement, I,1-3; Argument, 4; Index, I,321-323; II, 318-320.
Engravings as in 3a(i). "Books printed for . . . G. Pearch", I,324.
N.B. Cancels: vol.I, *A*1 hft; H1-K8, pp.97-144; S5-T3, pp.265-288; Y1-2, Index and advt.; vol.II, *A*1 hft; F1-G8, pp.65-96; X4-8, pp.311-320. New poems substituted for those by Akenside, Keate and Walpole. Reference to Dodsley's *Collection* on hft suppressed. Names of authors added in Indices. Catchwords: as in 3a(i), plus I,124, Such (for And); 264, EPISTLE (for ODE); II,88, They (for Thy).

3b. *Pearch's Collection, 4 vols, 1770*

Title-page as in 3(a) except for number of vols. (4), and date: M.DCC.LXX.
Half-titles: A Collection of Poems. The second edition. Vol.I (II).
          A Collection of Poems. Vol.III (IV).
8°. Vol.I: A^4 B-X^8 Y^4; *i-iv* i-iii *iv 1* 2-324 *325-328. A*1 hft.
    II: A^2 B-X^8 Y^2; *i-iv 1* 2-48 "65-80" 65-320 *321-324. A*1 hft.
    III: A^2 B-U^8 X^2; *i-iv 1* 2-138 "19" 140-160 "129" 162-206 "206" 208-252 "153" 254-304 *305-308. A*1 hft.
    IV: A-U^8 X^4; *1-5 6-323 324-328. A*1 hft. *324* blank.
Advertisement, I,i-iii; Argument, *iv*; Index, I,*325-328*; II,*321-324*; III,*305-308*; IV,*325-328*. Engravings, I,II, as in 3a; III,1, Mary Queen of Scots at the block (*Isaac Taylor del. et sculp.*); IV,5, man leaning against oak tree (*Isaac Taylor del. et sculp.*).
N.B. Date of imprint, II,III, without stops, MDCCLXX. Catchwords: I,214, To (for Tho'); II,30, Befor (for Before); 80, Bu (for But); 88, Thy (for The); 107, Heavenl (for Heavenly); 192, At (for Bring); 281, O (for Of); III,2, O (for Oh); 175, Where (for The); 181, Considerate (for Where); 250, No (for Nor); IV,15, KIM- (for ODE).

3c. *Pearch's Collection, 4 vols, 1775*

Title-page as in 3(a) except for imprint: London: Printed for G. Pearch, and sold by Joseph Johnson, St.Paul's Church-yard. MDCCLXXV.
Half-titles: A Collection of Poems; consisting of valuable pieces, not inserted in Mr. Dodsley's Collection, or published since. With several originals, by eminent writers. Vol.I (II, III, IV).

8°. Vol.I: A^2 a^4 B-X^8; *i-iv* 1-7 *8 1* 2-219 "120-121" 222-317 *318-320. A*1 hft.

II: A^2 B-X^8; *i-iv 1* 2-202 "103" 204-207 "108" 209-316 *317-320. A*1 hft.

III: A^2 B-X^8 Y^4; *i-iv 1* 2-220 "121" 222-324 *325-328. A*1 hft.

IV: A^2 B-X^8 Y^2; *i-iv 1* 2-310 "113" 312-316 *317-324. A*1 hft.

Dedication to Sir William Mayne, I,1-4(sig.a); Advertisement, 5-7; Argument, *8*; engravings as in 3b. Index, I,*318-320*; II,*317-320*; III,*325-328*; IV,*317-320*. Errata (for all four volumes), IV,*321*; advt for books "lately published by J. Johnson", *323-324*.

N.B. Cancels: II,C7 (so signed); P8 (signed P); IV, F6 (sø signed). Catchwords: II,178, VI.But (for IV.But); III,304, Tho' (for Exil'd). Misprints: III,126, DESENT (for DESCENT); IV,24, GANZONETTA (for CANZONETTA).

3d.   *Pearch's Collection, 4 vols, 1783*

Title-page as in 3(a) except for imprint: London: Printed by assignment from the executors of G. Pearch, for J. Dodsley, in Pall-Mall. (rule) M.DCC.LXXXIII. *Half-titles*: A Collection of Poems, intended as a Supplement to Mr. Dodsley's Collection. A new edition. With notes. Vol.I (II, III, IV).

8°. Vol.I: A^2 a^4 B-X^8 Y^4 Z^2; *i* ii-xi *xii 1* 2-329 *330-332. A*1 hft.

II: A^2 B-X^8; *i-iv 1* 2-316 *317-320. A*1 hft.

III: A^2 B-X^8 Y^5; *i-iv 1* 2-326 *327-330. A*1 hft.

IV: A^2 B-X^8 Y^3; *i-iv 1* 2-168 "139" 170-322 *323-326. A*1 hft.

Advertisement to the former editions, I,v-viii; Advertisement to the present edition, ix-xi; Argument, *xii.* Index, I,*330-332*; II,*317-320*; III,*327-330*; IV,*323-326.* Engravings as in 3b.

N.B. Biographical footnotes by editor (Isaac Reed) *passim.* Catchwords: III,103, Eterna (for Eternal); 185, LIF (for LIFE).

CONTENTS OF SUPPLEMENTS TO DODSLEY

THE POETICAL CALENDAR

Volume III (for March)

Volume VIII (for August)

Volume X (for October)

Volume XII (for December)

Volume I (variant b)

Additions

Omissions

Volume II (variant b)

Additions

Omissions

1770: Volume I, 2nd edition.

PEARCH'S COLLECTION

1775: Volume I.

Additions   Page

Volume IV.

PEARCH'S COLLECTION

1783: Volume II.

Additions   Page

Omissions

INDEX OF AUTHORS

Notes: 1. References with *asterisk indicate that the poem is anonymous, or with initials only, in that edition.
2. Titles in (brackets) indicate incorrect attributions.

Section A: Poems of known authorship

	F63	M67	M70	P68	P70	P75	P83
Akenside, Mark							
1. On the Winter-Solstice	i,12	274	185				
2. Friendship and Love[1]	*vi,107						
3. A Song[2]	*—,110						
4. Epistle to Curio				*ia,265		iii,36	iii,36
5. Love, an Elegy				iia,309		—,49	—,50
6. Ode to Sleep				—,314		—,54	—,55
7. A British Philippic						—,57	—,58
8. Hymn to Science						—,64	—,65
Alsop, Anthony							
1. Epistle to Sir J. Dolben						ii,296	ii,294
Anstey, Christopher							
1. On the Death of the Marquis of Tavistock					*iii,117	iii,161	iii,163
Armstrong, John							
1. Of Benevolence				ii,94			
Atterbury, Francis							
1. On a Fan	viii,74						
2. Ninth Ode of Horace, Bk.3	—,75						
3. Third Ode of Horace, Bk.4	—,76						
4. Verses on his Banishment	—,78						
Bacon, Francis, Viscount Verulam							
1. Parody on the Epigram of Posidippus	ii,68						
Bacon, Phanuel							
1. The Kite	iii,49						

---

1. New CBEL, ii, 637.
2. "By M.A." in text; Akenside in General Index, vol.xii.

	F63	M67	M70	P68	P70	P75	P83
Barclay, James							
1. The Tulip and Lily					*iii,171	iii,283	iii,285
2. The Invitation					*—,175	—,287	—,289
3. The Metamorphose					*—,178	—,289	—,291
4. The Sine Quo Non					*—,179	—,290	—,292
Barford, Richard							
1. The Great Shepherd						iii,138	iii,140
Beattie, James							
1. Retirement, an Ode					iv,74	iv,55	iv,55
2. The Triumph of Melancholy					—,77	—,58	—,58
3. Elegy occasioned by the Death of a Lady					—,86	—,67	—,67
4. The Hermit					*iii,47	—,71	—,71
5. Ode on Lord Hay's Birthday						—,73	—,73
Belsham, James							
1. Nothing	xi,9						
Berenger, Richard							
1. Verses to Mr. Dodsley		215					
Blacklock, Thomas							
1. Psalm CIV imitated	iii,78						
2. The Wish				ii,211	ii,207	ii,193	ii,194
3. Hymn to Fortitude				—,215	—,211	—,197	—,198
Bowden, Samuel							
1. The Hymn of Cleanthes	i,72						
Boyle, John, Earl of Cork							
1. Horace, Ode XIV, Book 2	ix,118						
Boyse, Samuel							
1. Deity	ii,9						
2. On Friendship[3]	*xi,118						
Bramston, James							
1. J. Bramston to Capt. Hinton	viii,94						
Brereton, Charlotte							
1. The Rattle	xi,14						

3. Chalmers, xiv,531.

	F63	M67	M70	P68	P70	P75	P83
Brerewood, Thomas							
1. Spring	iii,9				ii,94	ii,94	ii,94
2. Summer	vi,5				−,97	−,97	−,97
3. Autumn	ix,7	162			−,99	−,99	−,99
4. Winter	i,5				−,102	−,102	−,102
Brooke, Mrs. Frances							
1. Ode to Health					iv,93		
2. Ode ("O far remov'd")					−,95		
3. Ode to Friendship					−,96		
Broome, William							
1. The Oak and the Dunghill[4]	*ix,47						
Brown, John							
1. The Cure of Saul			279	ii,100	ii,104	ii,104	ii,104
2. Inscription at a Favourite Retirement				−,111	−,115	−,115	−,115
Browne, Isaac Hawkins							
1. The Fire-side	ix,14						
2. Ode to Health					*iii,199	ii,313	ii,315
Browne, Sir Thomas							
1. An Evening Hymn	xi,121						
Broxholm, Noel							
1. Horace, Ode xxx, Book 1	ix,119						
Buckingham, Duke of See Villiers, George							
Byrom, John							
1. A Divine Pastoral	xi,115						
Canning, George							
1. Epistle from William Lord Russell					iii,147	iii,188	iii,190
2. A Birth-day Offering					−,162	−,203	−,205
Carter, Elizabeth							
1. Ode to Melancholy				i,143	i,154	i,168	i,176
2. Ode ("With restless agitations")				−,147	−,158	−,172	−,180
3. Written at Midnight in a Thunderstorm				−,149	−,160	−,174	−,182
4. To ———				−,151	−,162	−,176	−,184

4. See Foxon B499.

	F63	M67	M70	P68	P70	P75	P83
Carter, Elizabeth (cont.)							
5. Written extempore on the Sea Shore				−,153	−,164	−,178	−,186
6. To Mrs. ———				−,154	−,165	−,179	−,187
7. To ———, occasioned by an Ode by Mrs. Phillips				−,156	−,167	−,181	−,189
8. A Night Piece				−,159	−,170	−,184	−,192
Cawthorne, James							
1. Abelard to Eloisa				i,1	i,1	i,1	i,1
2. To Miss ———						−,13	−,14
Charles I, King							
1. On a quiet Conscience	viii,66						
Chesterfield, Earl of See Stanhope, Philip Dormer							
Cheyne, George							
1. Answer to Dr. Wynter[5]	viii,87						
Cockfield, Joseph[6]							
1. Ode to Content					*iii,276		
2. Ode to Solitude[7]	*viii,19				*−,277		
3. Ode to Health					*−,278		
4. Epitaph on a Schoolfellow					−,280		
5. Inscription for a Hermitage[8]	*iv,11				*−,284		
6. Written at the Hermitage at Aldersbrook				*iib,317	*iv,132	*iv,117	*iv,117
7. Advice to a Shepherd					*−,133	*−,118	*−,118
8. Ode to Autumn[9]	*x,11				*−,134	*−,119	*−,119
9. Epitaph on a Peasant					*−,135	*−,120	*−,120
10. Psalm 137					*−,136		
11. The latter Part of Habakkuk, III					*−,137		
12. Verses wrote in an Alcove	*vi,9						
13. Written in an Alcove at Amwell[10]					*iv,179		

5. See Wynter, John.
6. Pearch gives nos.1-4 by "J—— C——"; nos.6-11 by "Mr. C——". *Shenstone's Miscellany*, ed. I.A. Gordon, 1952, gives nos.2, 3, 5, 11 by "Mr. J.C.", identified as Joseph Cockfield from Nichols, *Illustrations*, 1828, v,753-808, where Cockfield's letters include nos.6, 12, 13.
7. Pearch version considerably revised.
8. Pearch version revised and shortened with title "Inscription for a Roothouse".
9. Title in F63, "Farewell to the Country".
10. Attributed by Pearch to Langhorne (q.v.).

	F63	M67	M70	P68	P70	P75	P83
Cockfield, Joseph (cont.)							
14. (Sonnet on leaving B-r-n)[11]					*iii,281		
Collins, William							
1. Oriental Eclogues: Selim	xi,17	7	11	ii,1	ii,1	ii,1	ii,1
2. Oriental Eclogues: Hassan	—,20	12	14	—,4	—,4	—,4	—,4
3. Oriental Eclogues: Abra	—,24	15	17	—,8	—,8	—,8	—,8
4. Oriental Eclogues: Agib	—,27	18	20	—,11	—,11	—,11	—,11
5. Ode to Pity	—,31			—,17	—,17	—,17	—,17
6. Ode to Fear	—,33	21	23	—,31	—,31	—,31	—,31
7. Ode to Simplicity	—,36			—,19	—,19	—,19	—,19
8. Ode on the Poetical Character	—,39			—,34	—,34	—,34	—,34
9. Ode written in 1746	—,42						
10. Ode to Mercy	—,43			—,23	—,23	—,23	—,23
11. Ode to Liberty	—,45			—,24	—,24	—,24	—,24
12. Ode on the Death of Col. Ross	—,52						
13. Ode to Evening	—,55						
14. Ode to Peace	—,58			—,22	—,22	—,22	—,22
15. The Manners	—,59			—,38	—,38	—,38	—,38
16. The Passions	—,62	24	26	—,41	—,41	—,41	—,41
17. Epistle to Sir Thomas Hanmer	—,67						
18. Song from Cymbeline	—,74						
19. On the Death of Thomson	xii,104			—,15	—,15	—,15	—,15
20. Written on a Paper which contained Bride Cake				—,46	—,46	—,46	—,46
21. (To Miss Aurelia C——r)[12]	—,108						
Colman, George See Lloyd, Robert, 2, 3)							
Congreve, William							
1. Epistle to Lord Cobham	iii,108						
Conyers, Dr.							
1. On cutting down some trees	iv,111						

11. "By the same" as nos.1-4, according to P70; but actually by Thomas Percy (q.v.).
12. Inserted in James Hampton's account of the life and writings of Collins in F63 and repeated as "Collins' first production" as an appendix to Johnson's *Lives of the Poets*; but really by Dr. Swan (q.v.).

	F63	M67	M70	P68	P70	P75	P83
Cooper, John Gilbert							
1. Hymn to Health[13]	*iii,97						
2. The Genius of Britain[14]	*vi,105	*191	*150				
3. A Father's Advice to his Son[15]	*xi,76				iii,112	iii,156	iii,158
Cooper, T.							
1. Ode for the King's Birth-day	vi,112						
Cork, John, Earl of							
See Boyle, John							
Cotton, Nathaniel							
1. Solitude, a Song					iv,205		
2. To the Memory of the Duke of Bridgwater	ix,122				−,206		
Coventry, Francis							
1. Inscription for an Oak	vi,111						
Cowley, Abraham							
1. Force of Love	viii,80						
Cowper, Judith							
See Madan, Mrs.							
Cunningham, John							
1. Stanzas occasioned by the Forwardness of Spring[16]	*ii,3						
2. Corydon	iv,81	317	222				
3. Morning	−,83	310	214		iii,297		
4. Noon	−,85	312	216		−,299		
5. Evening	−,87	314	218		−,301		
6. On May	−,89				−,303		
7. Elegy on a Pile of Ruins	vii,10			ib,116	i,108	i,123	i,129
8. Pomona	−,109						
9. Content		316	220				
10. Melody		319	223				
Cunningham, Peter							
1. Ode to the New Year 1769					iii,79		
2. The Contented Philosopher					−,82	iii,279	iii,281

13. Chalmers, xv,516.
14. Chalmers, xv,517. An "Iambic Ode", different from Anon G1.
15. See note on "Winifreda" (Anon W1).
16. Chalmers, xiv,437.

	F63	M67	M70	P68	P70	P75	P83
Dalrymple, Hew							
1. Woodstock[17]				*ii,155	*ii,151	*ii,165	*ii,165
Dalton, John							
1. Descriptive Poem on the Mines at White-haven				i,23	i,23	i,37	i,39
2. Epistle to Viscount Beauchamp				−,43	−,43	−,57	−,60
3. Epistle to the Countess of Hertford				−,54	−,54	−,68	−,71
4. Some Thoughts on Building				−,64	−,64	−,78	−,82
Darwall, Mrs. See Whateley, Mary							
Davison, Francis							
1. Cupid's Pastime[18]		*150	*121				
Delany, Patrick							
1. A Song		219					
Delap, John							
1. Elegy I				i,77	i,77	i,91	i,95
2. Elegy II: To Sickness		107	90	−,81	−,81	−,95	−,99
Denis, Charles							
1. The Distribution of Gifts	i,97						
2. Alexander's Stick	−,99						
3. Jupiter and the Poet	−,102						
4. The Frog and the Rat	−,104						
5. The Young Widow	−,106						
6. The Adventurer and the Treasure	ii,97						
7. The Conqueror and the Old Woman	−,100						
8. Peace	ii,102						
9. Mercury and the Shades	−,106						
10. The Connoisseurs	−,110						
Denton, Thomas							
1. The House of Superstition			225	i,71	i,71	i,85	i,89
Devereux, Robert, Earl of Essex							
1. "Happy were he"	vii,113						

17. *N. & Q.*, 1st series, ix,589.
18. *Reliques*, i,336.

	F63	M67	M70	P68	P70	P75	P83
Devereux, Robert, Earl of Essex (cont.)							
2. The Buzzing Bee	−,114						
3. The Last Voyage	−,118						
Diaper, William							
1. The Dryads	ix,17						
Dobson, John							
1. Robin	ii,75						
Dodd, William							
1. The African Prince to Zara	*iv,13				iv,207	iv,217	iv,222
2. Zara to the African Prince	*−,20				−,214	−,224	−,230
3. Hymn to Hope					−,221		
4. Verses on a Moss Rose-bud					−,230		
Dodington, George Bubb, Baron Melcombe							
1. Verses sent to Dr. Young	viii,16			i,304	i,311	i,316	i,327
2. Verses under the Busto of Comus				−,305	−,312	−,317	−,329
Dodsley, Robert							
1. Melpomene[19]	*vi,37						
2. Answer to Mr. Berenger		216					
Dorset, Duke of							
See Sackville, Charles							
Duncombe, John							
1. The Feminead	vii,17				iv,186	iv,172	iv,176
2. An Evening Contemplation in a College	−,34						
3. Ode to the Duke of Newcastle	−,40						
4. Ode to James Yorke[20]	−,44				−,202	−,188	−,192
5. On Mr. Garrick	−,47						
6. Epistle from York	−,49						
7. Prologue spoken at the Charterhouse	−,53						
8. To the Author of Clarissa	−,55						
9. On the Campaign of 1759	−,59						

19. Chalmers, xv,348.
20. Misprinted "John" in F63 and P70.

	F63	M67	M70	P68	P70	P75	P83
Duncombe, John (cont.)							
10. To Colonel Clive	−,62						
11. On the Loss of HMS Ramillies	−,63						
12. Method of chusing a Mayor	−,65						
13. Voltaire to the Princess Amelia	−,67						
14. The King's Answer	−,69						
15. The Hertfordshire Grove[21]	*x,65						
16. The Middlesex Garden	*−,66						
17. Kensington-Gardens	*−,69						
18. Farewell to Hope	*−,73						
19. On a Lady's sending a Ribbon	*x,75						
20. On seeing Captain Cornwall's Monument	*−,77						
21. Prologue to Amalasont	*−,78						
22. Epigram on Narcissa	*−,79						
23. Epigram on a lady wounded by the author's sword	*−,80						
24. Epigram on the two naval victories	*−,80						
Duncombe, William							
1. To Daphne, on Valentine's Day	ii,79						
2. "Ad ornatissimam puellam" translated	xii,35						
3. The Faculties of the Soul	−,38						
4. Barrow's Latin verses translated	−,43						
Dyer, John							
1. Epistle to a Friend in Town	iii,112				i,153	i,167	i,175
Edwards, Samuel							
1. The Copernican System	iii,67						
Edwards, Thomas							
1. Sonnet to the Rev. Mr. Lawry	ix,112						
2. Sonnet to the Archbishop of Canterbury	xii,45						
3. Sonnet for the Root-house at Wrest					iv,49	ii,284	ii,282

21. Nos.15-24 signed "J.D."; identified as John Duncombe in *GM*, June 1786, p.451, which gives a full list of his writings.

	F63	M67	M70	P68	P70	P75	P83
Edwards, Thomas (cont.)							
4. Sonnet to Miss H.M[ulso].					−,50	−,285	−,283
5. Sonnet to W. Heberden, M.D.					−,51	−,286	−,284
6. Sonnet to Mr. Joseph Paice					−,52	−,287	−,285
7. Sonnet to the same					−,53	−,288	−,286
8. Sonnet to ———					−,54	−,289	−,287
9. Sonnet to the Deity					−,55	−,290	−,288
10. Sonnet to Matthew Barnard					−,56	−,291	−,289
Ekins, Jeffery							
1. On the Birth of a First Child						ii,315	
Ellis, John							
1. The Answer [to Mr. Mendez]		264					
Emily, Charles							
1. Death	xii,9			i,13	i,13	i,15	i,16
2. The Praises of Isis					iii,131	−,25	−,26
Essex, Robert, Earl of See Devereux, Robert							
Falconer, William							
1. Ode on the Duke of York's Departure		99					
Fawkes, Francis[22]							
1. On the Occasion of the Peace	*i,112						
2. Amaryllis	*ii,61						
3. The Honey-Stealer	*−,65						
4. Against Life	*−,66						
5. For Life	*−,67						
6. Passage from Petronius	*−,70						
7. Vernal Ode	*iii,3						
8. The XXXth Idyllium of Theocritus	*−,113						
9. Ode to Summer	*vi,3						
10. Autumnal Ode	*ix,3						
11. A Journey to Doncaster	*−,105						
12. Part of the Sixth Satire of Horace	*x,113						

22. Joint editor with Woty of the *Poetical Calendar*. All his contributions were anonymous, signed "F.F." (nos.1-8); "F" (13, 14); "A Gentleman of Cambridge" (9, 15); or nothing. See Chalmers, xvi,243-4 and 275-7 for nos.1, 4-7, 9-10, 12-15; xx (translations) for nos.2, 3, 8; and Bell's *Classical Arrangement of Fugitive Poetry*, 1790-97, ii,101, for no.11.

	F63	M67	M70	P68	P70	P75	P83
Fawkes, Francis (cont.)							
13. Parody on the City and Country Mouse	*−,116	175					
14. Horace, Epistle V, Book 1	*−,119						
16. Ode to Winter	xii,3						
Fitzgerald, Gerald							
1. The Academic Sportsman						iii,306	iii,308
Fletcher, Philip							
1. Truth at Court[23]	*iii,96						
Foote, Samuel							
1. Address to the Public		123	104				
Fordyce, James							
1. True Beauty				ib,277	i,281	i,286	i,297
Garrick, David							
1. Prologue upon Prologues		121	102				
2. Advice to the Marquis of Rockingham[24]		*139	*114				
3. Epilogue					iii,286		
Gay, John							
1. Wine	viii,35						
Gerrard, John							
1. Aminta					iv,277	iv,303	iv,309
2. Petherton-Bridge					−,282	−,308	−,314
3. Epistle from an Unfortunate Gentleman					−,285	−,311	−,317
4. A Song					−,290		
Glover, Richard							
1. Admiral Hosier's Ghost		154	123				
2. London				ii,48	ii,48	ii,48	ii,48
Glynn, Robert							
1. The Day of Judgment	xii,20						
Goldsmith, Oliver							
1. Edwin and Angelina[25]		55	49		iv,149	iv,133	iv,134
2. The Gift, to Iris		305	56				

23. *GM*, 1780, 123.
24. Garrick's *Poetical Works*, 1785, ii,514.
25. Under the title "The Hermit" in Pearch.

	F63	M67	M70	P68	P70	P75	P83
Grainger, James							
1. Bryan and Pereene[26]		*144	*115				
Graves, Richard							
1. Invitation to the Feathered Race					iii,107	iii,133	iii,135
2. Under an Hour Glass					—,109	—,135	—,137
3. On the Ancient City of Bath					—,110	—,136	—,138
Gray, Thomas							
1. Ode at the Installation of the Duke of Grafton					iii,93	iii,111	iii,112
2. A Long Story						—,116	—,117
3. The Fatal Sisters					—,98	—,122	—,124
4. The Descent of Odin					—,101	—,126	—,128
5. The Triumphs of Owen					—,105	—,130	—,132
6. Epitaph in a Country Churchyard	*viii,121					—,132	—,134
Greene, Edward Burnaby							
1. A Pastoral Hymn[27]	*xi,113						
Greville, Frances (Mrs)							
1. Prayer for Indifference	*vi,76	96	87	i,294	i,298	i,303	i,314
Greville, Fulke							
1. The Man of Sorrow	*ii,89			i,298	i,305	i,310	i,321
2. The Man of Pleasure	*—,92			—,304	—,308	—,313	—,324
Hammond, James							
1. Love Elegies I						iv,191	iv,195
2. Love Elegies II						—,193	—,197
3. Love Elegies III						—,195	—,199
4. Love Elegies IV[28]					iv,106	—,196	—,200
5. Love Elegies V						—,198	—,202
6. Love Elegies VI						—,200	—,204
7. Love Elegies VII[28]	viii,3				—,108	—,202	—,206
8. Love Elegies VIII						—,204	—,208
9. Love Elegies IX						—,205	—,209
10. Love Elegies X						—,207	—,211
11. Love Elegies XI						—,208	—,212
12. Love Elegies XII						—,209	—,213
13. Love Elegies XIII[28]					—,110	—,210	—,214
14. Love Elegies XIV						—,214	—,218
15. Love Elegies XV						—,215	—,219

26. *Reliques*, i,352.
27. E. B. Greene, *Poetical Essays*, 1771, p.74.
28. The three Elegies in P70 are numbered 1, 2, 3, though really 4, 7, 13.

	F63	M67	M70	P68	P70	P75	P83
Hardinge, Nicholas							
1. Dialogue in the Senate-House at Cambridge	ix,92						
Hardwicke, Earl of							
See Yorke, Philip							
Harington, Henry[29]							
1. Euthemia				*ib,123			
2. The Court of Discord				*—,131			
3. Slander, or the Witch of Wokey				*—,133	*i,139	*i,153	*i,161
Harington, John							
1. Sonnet on Isabella Markham[30]					iv,181	iv,167	iv,171
Harris, James							
1. Concord	xii,53						
Harte, Walter							
1. To the Earl of Chesterfield					iii,181		
2. Epitaph on Mrs. Mence					—,183		
Hartis, C.T.							
1. Ode written before the Long Vacation	vii,106						
Hawkesworth, John[31]							
1. Winter, an Ode[32]	*i,3				(*)iii,242	(*)iii,240	(*)iii,242
2. The Death of Arachne	*iii,33				*—,223	—,176	—,178
3. Life, an Ode	*—,41				—,143	—,184	—,186
4. Ode to Hope	*—,44						
5. The Origin of Doubt	*iv,60						
6. On Theological Enquiries	*—,63						
7. The Accident	*v,112						
8. To the Rev. Mr. Layng	*—,118						
9. Verses to the Rev. Mr. Warburton	*vi,63						
10. God is Love	*—,64						
11. Cloe's Soliloquy	*—,117						
12. The Devil-Painter	*—,118						
13. Song	*vii,122						

29. See *Reliques*, i,348, for nos.1 and 3; no.2 "by the same".
30. *Nugae Antiquae*, ed. H. Harington, 1769, p.129. See also Anon H5, T6.
31. Chalmers, *British Essayists*, 1823, xxiii, p.v-vi, lists Hawkesworth's contributions to *GM* (generally under the pseudonym of "Mr. Greville").
32. Nos.1, 15 and 17 were attributed to Johnson by Pearch and included in Bell's and Cooke's editions of Johnson's *Poetical Works*; though correctly identified as Hawkesworth's by Chalmers. See Nichol Smith, pp.462-3.

	F63	M67	M70	P68	P70	P75	P83
Hawkesworth, John (cont.)							
14. Thought from M. Antoninus	*viii,96						
15. Autumn, an Ode[32]	*ix,5				(*)iii,240	(*)iii,237	(*)iii,239
16. A Moral Thought					−,146	−,187	−,189
17. The Midsummer Wish[32]					(*)−,238	(*)−,236	(*)−,238
Hay, William							
1. Mount Caburn				ib,57			
Hayes, Daniel							
1. An Elegy						iii,299	iii,301
Heber, Reginald							
1. Elegy written among the Tombs in Westminster Abbey[33]						*ii,135	*ii,135
Hedges, T.							
1. T.H. to Sir Hans Sloane	viii,91						
Henley, Samuel							
1. Epigram to the Author of the note on Pope's Works					iii,34		
2. The Shaft					−,35	iii,298	iii,300
3. Iris to Philus					−,36		
4. Love Elegy					−,38		
5. Inscription under the Shade of a Lady					−,40		
6. Ode to Evening				i,315			
Hervey, James							
1. Imitation of Theocritus	viii,83						
2. Imitated from Casimir	−,84						
3. Imitation of Juvenal	−,85						
Hoole, John							
1. Monody to the Memory of Mrs. Woffington			*271	*iib,84	ii,85	ii,85	ii,85
Hudson, Thomas							
1. Ode to Liberty	vi,22			i,84	i,84	i,98	i,102
2. Ode to Fancy	−,26			−,88	−,88	−,102	−,106
3. Ode on True Greatness	−,30			−,91	−,91	−,105	−,109
4. Ode to Concord	−,33			−,94	−,94	−,108	−,112

32. Nos.1, 15 and 17 were attributed to Johnson by Pearch and included in Bell's and Cooke's editions of Johnson's *Poetical Works*; though correctly identified as Hawkesworth's by Chalmers. See Nichol Smith, pp.462-3.
33. Halkett & Laing, 1926, ii,147.

	F63	M67	M70	P68	P70	P75	P83
Hughes, John							
1. The Wandering Beauty	iv,112						
Hurd, Richard							
1. On the Peace of Aix				ii,297	ii,295	ii,281	ii,297
Hutchinson, Benjamin							
1. Marriage[34]						*ii,178	*ii,178
2. Kimbolton Park[35]					*iv,65	*iv,46	*iv,46
Irwin, Eyles							
1. Bedukah							ii,243
2. Eastern Eclogues: Alexis							−,259
3. Eastern Eclogues: Selima							−,264
4. Eastern Eclogues: Ramah							−,269
5. Eastern Eclogues: The Escape							−,275
Jago, Richard							
1. Labour and Genius						iii,208	iii,210
Jeffreys, George							
1. The Sixteenth of May	v,29						
Jenyns, Soame							
1. The Squire and the Parson[36]				*i,308	*i,315	*i,303	*i,302
Jerningham, Edward							
1. The Nun[37]		*299	*204				
2. Elegy written among the Ruins of an Abbey					ii,117	ii,117	ii,117
3. Il Latte					−,123	−,130	−,130
4. Amabella					iv,34	−,123	−,123
Johnson, Samuel[38]							
1. Prologue to Comus				i,306	i,313	iii,234	iii,236
2. An Ode	*iv,3				*iii,236		
3. The Winter's Walk	*i,17	208	164		*−,244	−,242	−,244
4. Song to Stella					*−,245	−,243	−,245
5. Evening Ode[39]	*ix,11				*−,246	−,244	−,246
6. The Natural Beauty					*−,247		

34. Halkett & Laing, iv,24.
35. "By the Rev. Mr. H.———"; Halkett & Laing, iii,218.
36. Chalmers, xvii,614.
37. Jerningham, *Poems*, 2 vols, 1786, i,24.
38. See Nichol Smith, pp.450-453. Nos.4-7 are classed as "of doubtful authorship"; nos.12-14 are really by John Hawkesworth (q.v.).
39. F63, "To Delia"; P70, "To Stella".

	F63	M67	M70	P68	P70	P75	P83
Johnson, Samuel (cont.)							
7. The Vanity of Wealth					*−,249	−,245	−,247
8. To Miss ——, on her network purse					*−,250		
9. Translation of the Latin Epitaph on Sir T. Hanmer					*−,251		
10. To Miss ——, on her playing the harpsichord					*−,253	iii,247	−,249
11. Epitaph on Claudius Phillips		209	165				
12. (Winter, an Ode)					−,242	−,246	−,242
13. (Autumn, an Ode)					−,240	−,237	−,239
14. (The Midsummer Wish)					−,238	−,236	−,238
Jones, Lewis							
1. Reflections at an Inn	iii,99						
Keate, George							
1. The Alps				ia,107			
2. Lady Jane Grey				−,125			
3. The Ruins of Netley Abbey				−,138			
4. Ancient and Modern Rome[40]				*iia,72			
5. To a Lady going to bathe in the Sea					iii,72	iii,269	iii,271
6. Prologue to King John					−,74	−,271	−,273
7. Epilogue to King John					−,76	−,273	−,275
Kennett, Basil							
1. On the Illness of Dr. Turner	ix,59						
King, Charles							
1. Receipt for Eau de Vie		308	212				
Langhorne, John							
1. To a Redbreast	viii,58						
2. Caesar's Dream		288	199				
3. Ode to the River Eden				i,312	iv,166	iv,150	iv,154
4. On the Duchess of Mazarin					−,169	−,153	−,157
5. The Tulip and Myrtle					−,173		
6. Rural Simplicity					−,176		
7. (Written on a Chinese Temple)[41]					−,179		

40. Keate, *Poetical Works*, 2 vols, 1781, i,13.
41. Attributed to Langhorne by Pearch, but not found in Cooke's or Park's editions of his poems. The same, apart from the title, as "Written in an Alcove at Amwell" by Joseph Cockfield (q.v.).

	F63	M67	M70	P68	P70	P75	P83
Langhorne, John (cont.)							
8. Written on another Temple					−,179		
9. Line occasioned by Lord Lyttelton's Verses					−,180		
Leapor, Mary							
1. The Month of August[42]	*viii,7						
Lloyd, Robert							
1. The Cit's Country Box	*iv,102	62	57				
2. Ode to Obscurity[43]	*vi,46						
3. Ode to Oblivion[43]	*−,52						
4. Ode to Genius[44]	*vii,7						
5. The Actor		67	61				
6. To the Moon					iv,97		
7. Ballad ["Ye Shepherds"]					−,102		
8. (Ballad: "Hark! Hark!)[45]					−,104		
Locke, John							
1. On the Peace of 1654	viii,71						
2. To Oliver Cromwell	−,73						
Lockman, John							
1. The Muses, Mercury and Fame[46]	*viii,17						
Lowth, Robert							
1. Ad Ornatissimam Puellam	xii,34						
2. The Genealogy of Christ					iv,114	iv,77	iv,77
Lyttelton, George, Lord[47]							
1. Virtue and Fame	*viii,11						
2. Letter to the Earl of H[ardwic]ke	*−,14						
3. Character of Thomson	*xii,106						
Madan, Mrs. Judith (Cowper)[48]							
1. The Progress of Poetry	iii,17						
2. To the Memory of Mr. Hughes	−,29						

42. Mrs. Leapor, *Poems on Several Occasions*, 1748, p.34.
43. Chalmers, xv,93-4; from *Two Odes* (parodies) by Lloyd and George Colman.
44. Chalmers, xv,137.
45. See note on Moore, Edward, 3.
46. "By the author of the Epistle to the Rt. Hon. Arthur Onslow" (*GM*, May 1761, p.232), i.e. John Lockman (see *MR*, xxiv,444, June 1761).
47. "By Lord L——n"; Chalmers, xiv,183.
48. See note on Pattison, William, i.

	F63	M67	M70	P68	P70	P75	P83
Mallet, David							
1. William and Margaret		77	71				
2. A Fragment		81			i,97	i,111	i,115
3. Zephir		84	75				
4. On the Death of Lady Anson					−,101	−,115	−,120
5. Edwin and Emma		92	82		−,104	−,118	−,123
Marlowe, Christopher							
1. The Shepherd's Invitation[49]	ii,53	*147	*118		iii,290		
Marriott, James							
1. Laura			296	ii,300	ii,298	iv,9	iv,9
2. Rinaldo and Armida				iib,311	−,307	−,18	−,18
3. Sacred Ode				−,313	−,309	−,20	−,20
4. Inscription on a Hermitage				−,316	−,312	−,23	−,23
5. Canzonetta					−,313	−,24	−,24
6. The Valetudinarian					iv,1	−,1	−,1
7. The Royal Voyage					−,13	−,25	−,25
8. Ode on Death					−,16	−,28	−,28
9. Inscription on a Monument					−,21	−,33	−,33
10. To a Lady sitting for her Picture					−,22	−,34	−,34
11. Elegy on the Death of a Young Lady					−,24	−,36	−,36
12. The Academic					−,28	−,40	−,40
Mason, William							
1. Elegy on Lady Coventry		1	1				
2. Il Bellicoso					iii,86	i,204	i,213
3. Il Pacifico				i,180	i,190	−,211	−,220
4. On the Death of his Wife					−,196	−,217	−,226
5. Epitaph on Miss Drummond						−,218	−,227
6. Elegy to a Young Nobleman				−,186	−,197	−,219	−,228
7. Isis, an Elegy		294	6	−,189	−,200	−,222	−,231
Melcombe, Lord							
See Dodington, George Bubb							
Melmoth, William							
1. The Transformation of Lycon					ii,128	ii,142	ii,142
2. A Tale					−,135	−,149	−,149
3. Epistle to Sappho					−,137	−,151	−,151

49. Title in Mendez (as in *Reliques*) is "The Passionate Shepherd to his Love".

	F63	M67	M70	P68	P70	P75	P83
Mendez, Jael (Mrs. Pye)[50]							
1. On Mr. Walpole's House at Strawberry-Hill		*223					
Mendez, Moses							
1. The Thirteenth Book of Virgil		227					
2. Account of his Journey to Ireland		257	172				
3. To Mr. S. Tucker		267	179				
4. Imitation of Spenser	v,35						
5. The Seasons: Spring	—,37		305	ii,234	ii,230	ii,216	ii,217
6. The Seasons: Summer	—,41		308	—,237	—,233	—,219	—,220
7. The Seasons: Autumn	—,44		310	—,241	—,237	—,223	—,224
8. The Seasons: Winter	—,48		313	—,244	—,240	—,226	—,227
Merrick, James							
1. The Ignorance of Man				ib,141	i,142	i,156	i,164
2. The Trials of Virtue					—,144	—,158	—,166
3. Verses in the Persic Language					—,147	—,161	—,169
4. A Hymn to the Creator	i,75				—,148	—,162	—,170
5. The Lord's Prayer paraphrased					—,152	—,166	—,174
Mickle, William Julius							
1. Mary Queen of Scots					*iii,1	iii,1	iii,1
2. Hengist and Mey					*—,11	—,13	—,13
3. Knowledge					*—,19	—,21	—,21
4. Pollio				*i,232	*—,28	—,30	—,30
Mills, Andrew Hervey							
1. Allen and Ella[51]	*iii,119			*i,316	*i,320	*ii,308	*ii,312
2. The Lover and the Friend[52]					*ii,314		
Milton, John							
1. Sonnet on May Morning	v,28						
2. (Sonnet upon the Plague)[53]	viii,67						
3. (Fragment from the Italian)[54]	—,68						

50. By "Miss M———", i.e. Mendez, though by 1767 she had been married twice. Published in *Poems by a Lady*, 1767, together with Walpole's reply (q.v.). Reprinted 1771; "second edition" 1772, by "Mrs. Hampden Pye", the name of her second husband.

51. Title in F63 "Colin and Lucy" (no connection with Tickell's ballad), under which it was surreptitiously published in 1755, according to a note in Mills's *Bagatelles*, 1767, p.32, where it appears with its new title. See Halkett & Laing, ii,370.

52. Written before Edward Moore's poem of the same title, according to a note in *Bagatelles*, p.1.

53. See Ault, 373-4; an imitation by Pope.

54. Paraphrase of Milton's Italian Canzone.

	F63	M67	M70	P68	P70	P75	P83

Moore, Anthony
  1. Soliloquy in a Country
     Churchyard
  2. Elegy written among
     some Ruins in
     Cornwall[55]
	ii,49
	
	viii,88						

Moore, Edward
  1. The Poet and his Patron
  2. The Wolf, Sheep and
     Lamb
  3. Ballad ("Hark! hark!")[56]
		278
		
		281
			189
			
			192
					
					iv,104		

Moss, Thomas 1. The Beggar[57]						*iii,322	*iii,324

Mulso, Hester (Mrs.
    Chapone)
  1. Sonnet to a Robin
     Redbreast[58]
					*iii,275		

Murphy, Arthur 1. Prologue					iii,285		

Ogilvie, John
  1. Ode to Melancholy
  2. Ode to the Genius of
     Shakespeare
  3. Ode to Time
  4. Ode to Sleep
  5. Ode to Evening
  6. Ode to Innocence
  7. A Song
			
			290
				ii,113
				
				−,118
				−,124
				−,130
				−,135
				−,141
					
					iii,170		

Onely, Richard 1. The Charge of Cyrus				i,238	i,242	i,264	i,274

Panting, Stephen
  1. Four Elegies: Morning
  2. Four Elegies: Noon
  3. Four Elegies: Evening
  4. Four Elegies: Midnight
	viii,20
	−,24
	−,28
	−,31						

55. No.1 is by "the Rev. Mr. Moore of Cornwall"; no.2 by "Mr. Moore". The latter appears in Bell's edition of the poetical works of *Edward* Moore, but not in his own collection of *Poems, Fables and Plays*, 1756, nor in Johnson's or Chalmers' series. As it is on a Cornish subject, it clearly belongs to "Mr. Moore of Cornwall", i.e. Anthony Moore, Vicar of Stratton, Cornwall, who regularly wrote on local themes (see Biographical Notes).
56. Chalmers, xiv,221. Mistakenly attributed by Pearch to Robert Lloyd, owing to its appearance "by the same" in Lloyd's *St. James's Magazine*, i,207.
57. See *GM*, lx (1790), 972; lxx (1800), 41.
58. "By Miss M———o"; see *Miscellanies in Prose and Verse*, by Mrs. Chapone (née Mulso), 1755, p.133.

	F63	M67	M70	P68	P70	P75	P83
Parsons, Philip							
1. Inscription in an Arbour					*iii,78	iii,275	iii,277
2. Absence					*iv,90	—,276	—,278
Pattison, William							
1. Abelard to Eloisa[59]	iv,27						
2. Rosamund to Henry	—,34						
3. Henry to Rosamund	—,45						
Pearson, Thomas							
1. Colin and Nancy						*iv,244	iv,250
2. A Pastoral Ballad						*—,247	—,253
3. The Throstle's Elegy						*—,250	—,256
4. Epistle to a Lady						*—,253	—,259
5. On Avaro						*—,258	—,264
6. On a Musical Lady						*—,259	—,265
7. An Expostulation						*—,259	—,265
8. The Morning Walk						*—,261	—,267
9. Epitaph on a Lady who died at Calcutta						*—,264	—,270
Pennington, Miss							
1. The Copper Farthing	x,48						
Penny, Mrs. Anne							
1. On the Royal Nuptials[60]	*i,109						
2. To Samuel Johnson	vii,81						
3. Anningait and Ajutt	—,82						
Percy, Thomas							
1. Sonnet on leaving B—x—n[61]					*iii,281	*iii,296	*iii,298
2. Sonnet to a Lady of indiscreet Virtue[62]					*—,289	*—,297	*—,299
Philips, Ambrose							
1. A Description of Winter	i,7						
Philips, John							
1. The Fall of Chloe's Jordan[63]	iv,107						
Pinnell, Peter							
1. Trust in God	i,81						

59. Mistakenly attributed to Mrs. Madan in *Poems by Eminent Ladies*, 1755; see Courtney, 83.
60. "By Mrs. P——" in text; "Mrs. Penny" in General Index, vol.xii.
61. "By J[ohn] C[ockfield]" in P70, but changed to "Dr. P——" in P75. See next.
62. "By T—— P——" in P70; "By the same" i.e. Dr. P——, P75. First published in Anna Williams' *Miscellanies*, 1766, and identified as Percy's by Hazen, *Samuel Johnson's Prefaces and Dedications*, 1937, p.214.
63. Published anonymously, 1713, as *The Memorable Fall of Chloe's P——s Pot*. Attribution to Philips in *Poetical Calendar* accepted by M.G. Lloyd Thomas, *The Poems of John Philips*, Blackwell, 1927.

	F63	M67	M70	P68	P70	P75	P83
Pinnell, Peter (cont.)							
2. On the Death of Lady Shaw	−,88						
3. A Sick Man's Address to his Candle	−,90						
4. Advice to a Young Lady	−,91						
5. To a Lady, asking my opinion of friendship	−,92						
Pitt, Christopher							
1. Dialogue between the Poet and his Servant	x,81	170	139				
2. To John Pitt, Esq.	−,86						
3. To Mr. Spence	−,88						
4. To Mr. Lowth	−,92						
5. Epistle to Mr. Spence	−,95						
6. The Invitation	−,98						
7. Ode to John Pitt, Esq.	−,100						
8. Ode to the same	−,103						
9. On Mrs. Walker's Poems	−,105						
10. Verses on a flowered carpet	−,106						
11. On the same	−,107						
12. The Art of Preaching	−,108						
13. Epitaph on his father, mother and brother	−,111						
14. Epitaph on Dr. Keil	−,112						
Pope, Alexander							
1. To the Author of a Panegyric on Mrs. Butler[64]	xii,60						
2. Inscription in a Grotto	−,61						
3. Verses on reading "A Fit of the Spleen"	−,62						
4. Verses left at Adderbury	−,63						
5. To the Duke of Argyle[64]	−,64						
6. Sonnet upon the Plague[65]	viii,67						
Portal, Abraham							
1. A Morning Elegy	xii,65						
2. An Evening Elegy	−,69						
3. Friendship	−,72						
4. Eliza's Wedding Day	−,75						
Porteus, Beilby							
1. Death					iii,49		

64. First ascribed to Pope here; considered dubious by Ault, pp.458(1);422(5).
65. See note on Milton, 2.

	F63	M67	M70	P68	P70	P75	P83
Potter, Robert							
1. Farewell Hymn to the Country	v,51						
2. Holkham				ii,263	ii,259	ii,245	ii,230
3. Kymber					iii,184		
Powys, Thomas							
1. A Morning Soliloquy on Deafness					*iv,147	iii,294	iii,296
Pratt, Samuel Jackson							
1. The Partridges						iii,292	iii,294
Raleigh, Sir Walter							
1. The Nymph's Answer	ii,55				iii,292		
2. A Poem	—,57				—,293		
3. The Silent Lover	vi,55						
Ramsay, Allan							
1. The Eagle and the Robin[66]		*291	*202				
Richardson, Mr.							
1. Ode to a Singing Bird					iv,141	iv,130	iv,131
Roberts, William Hayward							
1. The Poor Man's Prayer		*209	*165	*ii,271	*ii,267	ii,253	ii,238
Robertson, Rev. Mr.							
1. Sweetness					iii,202		
2. To Florella					—,205		
3. Barreaux's Sonnet translated					—,206		
Sackville, Charles, Duke of Dorset							
1. Arno's Vale					iv,59	ii,294	ii,292
2. Britain's Isle					—,60	—,295	—,293
Savage, Richard							
1. Verses on Lady Tyrconnel						iii,261	iii,263
2. The Bastard						—,265	—,267
Schomberg, Ralph							
1. Ode on the Rebellion of 1745				ii,168	ii,164		

66. Attribution to "Mr. Archibald Scott" taken from *The Union*, 1753; originally from Allan Ramsay's *Ever Green*, 1724, where it is signed "Ar.Scot". Sometimes ascribed to Johnson, but really by Ramsay himself (see Nichol Smith, 470).

	F63	M67	M70	P68	P70	P75	P83
Scott, Archibald							
See Ramsay, Allan							
Scott, James							
1. Every Man the Architect of his own Fortune		29	31				
2. Heaven				ii,180	ii,177		
3. Ode to the Muse				—,207	—,203	iii,69	iii,70
4. Ode to Friendship						—,73	—,74
5. Ode to Miss B——						—,76	—,77
6. Ode on Sleep				—,193	—,189	—,79	—,80
7. Ode to Pleasure		42	44	—,197	—,193	—,83	—,84
8. Ode on Despair				—,202	—,198	—,88	—,89
9. Ode to Wisdom						—,93	—,94
10. Spousal Hymn					iv,41	—,97	—,98
11. The Vanity of Human Life						—,105	—,106
Scott, John							
1. Elegy written at the Approach of Spring	*iii,5			*i,249	i,253	iv,87	iv,87
2. Elegy written in the Hot Weather				*—,253	—,257	—,91	—,91
3. Elegy written in the Harvest				*—,256	—,260	—,94	—,94
4. Elegy written at the Approach of Winter				*—,261	—,265	—,99	—,99
5. Hymn from Psalm VIII	*i,80				—,269	—,103	—,103
6. Elegy written at Amwell						—,104	—,104
7. Winter Prospects in the Country					*iv,124	—,108	—,108
8. Hymn occasioned by Psalm 65	*—,79				*—,126	—,110	—,110
9. Apology for Retirement					*—,127	—,111	—,111
10. Sonnet to Retirement					*—,128	—,112	—,112
11. Sonnet to Delia					*—,129	—,113	—,113
12. Sonnet to Britannia					*—,130	—,114	—,114
13. On reading Mrs. Macaulay's History					*—,131	—,115	—,115
14. Sonnet on Arbitrary Government					*iii,283	—,116	—,116
Shaw, Cuthbert							
1. Monody to the Memory of a Young Lady					iii,208	iii,219	iii,221
2. Evening Address to a Nightingale					—,218	—,229	—,232
Sheills, Robert[67]							
1. The Power of Beauty				*i,161	*i,172	i,186	i,194

67. Dr. Johnson's amanuensis, usually spelt "Shiels".

	F63	M67	M70	P68	P70	P75	P83
Shepherd, Richard							
1. Aristotle's Paean				i,278	i,282	i,287	i,298
2. Ode to Ambition			249	−,280	−,284	−,289	−,300
3. Ode to the Atheist				−,283	−,287	−,292	−,303
4. Ode to Melancholy				−,285	−,289	−,294	−,305
5. Ode on Envy				−,288	−,292	−,297	−,308
6. Ode to Health			251	−,290	−,294	−,299	−,310
Smart, Christopher							
1. Prologue to the Grateful Fair	iv,121						
2. On the 5th of December[68]	*xii,8						
3. Ode against Ill-Nature				ii,223	ii,219	ii,205	ii,206
4. Ode on St. Cecilia's Day				−,226	−,222	−,208	−,209
5. On the Eternity of the Supreme Being					iv,293		
6. On the Immensity of the Supreme Being					−,299		
7. On the Omniscience of the Supreme Being					−,305		
8. On the Power of the Supreme Being					−,312		
9. On the Goodness of the Supreme Being					−,318		
Smith, Caleb							
1. Epitaph upon his Wife		214	170				
Smollett, Tobias							
1. The Tears of Scotland[69]		*285	*196				
2. Ode to Independence						iv,121	iv,121
3. Ode to Sleep					*iv,138	−,127	−,128
4. Ode to Mirth					*−,139	−,128	−,129
Somervile, William							
1. To Lady Anne Coventry	iii,103						
2. Epistle to Mr. Thomson	−,106						
Spence, Joseph							
1. On the Royal Nuptials	iv,93						
Stanhope, Philip Dormer, Earl of Chesterfield							
1. On Mr. Nash's Picture					*iv,57	*ii,292	ii,290
2. On the Duchess of Richmond					*−,58	*−,293	−,291

68. Chalmers, xvi,23.
69. Chalmers, xv,585.

	F63	M67	M70	P68	P70	P75	P83
Stevenson, John Hall							
Fables for Grown							
Gentlemen: [70]							
1. The River with a							
Petition	*x,17						
2. The Phoenix and her							
Lovers	*—,21						
3. The Ducklings and the							
Wise Birds	*—,24						
4. The Fighting Cock and							
the Craven	*—,27						
5. The Dog and the Cat	*—,30						
6. The Spider and the Fly	*—,33						
7. The Wild Ducks and							
the Water-Spaniel	*—,36						
8. The Advice of an old							
Spaniel	*—,41						
Stevenson, William							
1. The Theory of Tears	ix,51						
Stone, Jerom							
1. Albin and the Daughter							
of Mey		47					
Swan, John							
1. To Miss Aurelia							
C——r [71]	(*)xii,108						
Thomas, Mrs. Elizabeth							
1. To William Shenstone,							
Esq. [72]		*115					
Thompson, William							
1. Hymn to May	v,1						
2. Garden Inscriptions: I.							
On Spenser's Faerie							
Queene	viii,97						
3. —— II. On Spenser's							
Shepherd's Calendar	—,98						
4. ——III. In Shakes-							
peare's Walk	—,99						
5. —— IV. In Milton's							
Alcove	—,100						

70. "By J—— H—— S——, Esq." i.e. John Hall Stevenson (New CBEL, ii,685).
71. Mistakenly attributed here to Collins (q.v.) owing to the confusion of two poems on weeping ladies in *GM*, 1739. This one, signed "Amasius", appeared in January, p.41; Collins' "Sonnet" in October, p.545, signed "Delicatulus". In 1780 Johnson told Nichols, "Amasius was at that time the poetical name of Dr. Swan, who translated Sydenham". (Hill, ii,130).
72. Sent to Shenstone in 1761 under the pseudonym "Cotswouldia"; identified by Marjorie Williams, *The Letters of William Shenstone*, 589n, as Elizabeth, wife of the Rev. John Thomas, of Notgrove, Glos.

	F63	M67	M70	P68	P70	P75	P83
Thompson, William (cont.)							
6. —— V. In the same [*Latin*]	−,100						
7. —— VI. On Laurel Hill, to Pope	−,101						
8. —— VII. In Chaucer's Boure	−,103						
9. —— VIII. At the end of the Canal	−,104						
10. —— IX. At the same [*Latin*]	−,106						
11. —— X. At the same	−,107						
12. —— XI. In Golden Grove	−,108						
13. —— XII. In Cowley's Shade	−,110						
14. —— XIII. Under Addison's Picture, on the Mount	−,112						
15. —— XIV. Another, underneath	−,113						
16. —— XV. On a Mount, under Virgil's Picture	−,113						
17. —— XVI. Under his Eclogues, by the Cascade	−,114						
18. —— XVII. Beneath a Vine, under Horace's Picture	−,115						
19. —— XVIII. Over Thomson's Seasons	−,117						
20. —— XIX. In an Apple-tree, over Philips' Cyder	−,118						
21. —— XX. Over Young's Night Thoughts	−,119						
22. Gratitude	xii,97						
Thornton, Bonnell							
1. Ode on St. Cecilia's Day		134	109				
Thrale, Mrs. Hester							
1. The Three Warnings					iii,258	iii,252	iii,254
Tickell, Thomas							
1. To the Author of the Spectator	i,18						
2. To Mr. Addison on Rosamund	−,21						
3. To the same, on Cato	−,24						
4. The Royal Progress	−,26						

	F63	M67	M70	P68	P70	P75	P83
Tickell, Thomas (cont.)							
5. Ode on Earl Stanhope's Voyage	−,32						
6. Prologue to the University of Oxford	−,34						
7. Thoughts occasioned by King Charles's Picture	−,36						
8. To Apollo, making love	−,39	226	171				
9. The Fatal Curiosity	−,40						
10. To a Lady, with the Phoenix	−,41						
11. Description of the Phoenix	−,42						
12. Verses to Mrs. Lowther	−,48						
13. To a Lady, with flowers	−,49						
14. On a Lady's Picture	−,51						
15. Part of the Fourth Book of Lucan	−,52						
16. To a Lady before Marriage	−,57	118	99				
17. A Poem in Praise of the Horn-Book	−,61						
18. On the Queen's rebuilding the Black Prince's lodgings	iii,117						
Vernon, William							
1. The Parish Clerk						ii,186	ii,186
Verulam, Lord							
See Bacon, Francis							
Villiers, George, Duke of Buckingham							
1. To a Lady, with a Pair of Gloves					iv,64	*ii,302	*ii,301
Walpole, Horace							
1. Epitaph on King Theodore[73]	*ix,123						
2. To the Authoress of some lines on Strawberry-Hill[74]		225					
3. Verses in Memory of King Henry VI[75]				*ia,97			

73. Hazen, *Bibliography of the Strawberry Hill Press*, 1973, 164.
74. See note on Mendez, Jael.
75. Nos.3-7, "By the Hon. H.W. Esq." See Hazen, *Bibliography of Horace Walpole*, 1973, pp.42-3.

	F63	M67	M70	P68	P70	P75	P83
Walpole, Horace (cont.)							
4. Inscription for the Neglected Column at Florence				*—,101			
5. The Entail				*—,103			
6. Portrait of Earl Granville				*—,105			
7. Sonnet to Lady Mary Coke				*—,106			
Warton, Joseph							
1. Ode to Liberty				ii,247	ii,243	ii,229	
2. Ode to Health				—,250	—,246	—,232	
3. Ode to Superstition				—,252	—,248	—,234	
4. Ode to a Gentleman on his Travels				—,254	—,250	—,236	
5. Ode against Despair				—,257	—,253	—,239	
6. Ode to the Nightingale				—,259	—,255	—,241	
7. Ode to a Lady who hates the Country				—,260	—,256	—,242	
8. Ode to Solitude				—,262	—,258	—,244	
Warton, Thomas[76]							
1. The Triumph of Isis			231	i,194	i,205	i,227	i,236
2. Newmarket	*x,54		240	—,204	—,214	—,236	—,246
3. On the Death of King George II	ii,81			—,213	—,223	—,245	—,255
4. On the Marriage of King George III				—,217	—,227	—,249	—,259
5. On the Birth of the Prince of Wales				—,221	—,231	—,253	—,263
6. Ode for Music				—,225	—,235	—,257	—,267
7. Ode written at the Approach of Summer[77]				*ib,265	*—,270	*—,275	*—,285
8. Five Pastoral Eclogues:[78] Lycas and Alphon				*ii,274	*ii,272	*ii,258	
9. ——: Acis and Alcyon				*—,279	*—,277	*—,263	
10. ——: Eclogue III				*—,283	*—,281	*—,267	
11. ——: Mycon and Philanthes				*—,287	*—,285	*—,271	
12. ——: Corin and Calistan				*—,292	*—,290	*—,276	
13. Ode to Pleasure[79]	*iii,47						
Wesley, Samuel (senior)							
1. Eupolis' Hymn[80]	*i,66						

76. See note on "Ode to Horror", Anon O5.
77. Chalmers, xviii,105.
78. See Foxon W245·5.
79. Autograph MS. in the library of Trinity College, Oxford; anonymously published in Dodsley's *Museum*, 1746, ii,50.
80. *DNB*, Wesley, Samuel (1662-1735).

	F63	M67	M70	P68	P70	P75	P83
West, Gilbert							
1. The Hymn of Cleanthes				i,68	i,68	i,82	i,86
2. Inscription in a Summer-house	viii,120			−,232	−,71	−,85	−,89
Wharton, Philip, Duke of							
1. On the Banishment of Cicero	xi,5						
2. On Bishop Atterbury's Preaching	−,7						
Whateley, Mary							
1. The Pleasures of Contemplation					iii,120	iii,164	iii,166
2. Liberty					−,124	−,168	−,170
3. Hymn to Solitude					−,126	−,171	−,173
4. Ode to May					−,129	−,174	−,176
Whitehead, Paul							
1. The Gymnasiad[81]	*viii,45						
Whitehead, William							
1. Ode for the New Year 1763	ii,86						
2. Ode for his Majesty's Birth-day	vii,120						
3. More Night Thoughts[82]	*xii,102						
4. Verses to the People of England		110	93				
5. A Charge to the Poets		125					
6. On Nobility						iv,231	iv,237
7. The Enthusiast				ib,137	ii,307	−,240	−,246
Wither, George							
1. The Shepherd's Resolution		158	126				
2. The Steadfast Shepherd		159	128				
Wodhull, Michael							
1. The Equality of Mankind					iv,231	iv,265	iv,271
Wooddeson, Richard							
1. The Lass of Isleworth Mill	xi,80						

81. "By Mr. P.W."; Chalmers, xvi,213.
82. Published in *GM*, Sept.1747, as "New Night Thoughts on Death, by Mr. Wh———"; identified by the Rev. William Cole (BL, MS Add.5832, f.144).

	F63	M67	M70	P68	P70	P75	P83
Woodhouse, James							
1. The Complaint[83]	*iii,86						
Woty, William[84]							
1. Ode on Darkness	*i,117						
2. January, an Ode	*—,119						
3. Ode to February	*ii,1						
4. The Bacchanalian	*—,95						
5. March, an Ode	*iii,1						
6. To Charity	*—,84						
7. April, an Ode	*iv,1						
8. Spring, an Ode	—,5						
9. Hymn on the Approach of May	*—,113						
10. Ode to Health	*—,116						
11. The Moonlight Night	*v,32						
12. Ode on Health	*vi,10						
13. Song	*—,12	*183	*149				
14. Ode to Evening	*—,13						
15. Song in Praise of Women	*—,116						
16. Hymn to the Morning	*vii,3						
17. Poem on a Pin	ix,63	165	134				
18. The Decline of Autumn	*x,5						
19. To Winter	xii,5	199	155				
Wright, Mrs. Mehetabel							
1. A Mother's Soliloquy	vi,79						
2. To the Memory of Varo	—,80						
3. To the Memory of a Sister	—,82						
4. The Lucid Interval	—,84						
5. Farewell to the World	—,85						
6. The Picture	—,88						
7. Epitaph on Herself	—,89						
Wynter, John							
1. Dr. Wynter to Dr. Cheyne	viii,86						

83. Printed under the title "Spring", with several changes, in Woodhouse's *Poems on Sundry Occasions*, 1764, with the complaint that it was "imperfectly printed in the Poetical Calendar ... without his knowledge or the compilers even mentioning to whom they were obliged".

84. As joint editor with Francis Fawkes, Woty contributed poems as (a) "Mr. Woty": nos.8, 17, 19; (b) "W.W.": nos.1, 2, 6, 15, 16, 18; (c) "W.": nos.3, 5, 7; (d) anonymous: nos.4, 9, 10, 11, 12, 13, 14. Woty's collections, *Shrubs of Parnassus*, 1760, *Blossoms of Helicon*, 1763, and *Poetical Works*, 2 vols, 1770, contain the seven anonymous poems and two of the "W.W." pieces. The other "W.W." items can therefore be assigned to him, as also the "W." poems on the analogy of his fellow-editor, who signed his contributions "F.F." or simply "F."

	F63	M67	M70	P68	P70	P75	P83
Yalden, Thomas 　1. To Sir Humphrey 　　Mackworth	iv,65						
Yonge, Sir William 　1. The Cause of 　　Inconstancy[85]	*xi,111						
Yorke, Philip, Earl of 　**Hardwicke** 　1. Addition extempore 　　to the verses to Lady 　　Egremont[86]	*viii,13						

85. Nichols, *Select Collection of Poems*, 8 vols, 1780, vi,255.
86. See Lyttelton, Lord, 2.

Section B. Authors with unidentified initials, etc.

	F63	M67	M70	P68	P70	P75	P83
S.B. Esq.							
1. To Colonel R———s					iii,41		
2. To A Lady, with an Etui					—,44		
3. To the same, after receiving a watch					—,45		
4. To the same, with Shenstone's Works					—,46		
Countess of C———							
1. The Fairy's Answer to Mrs. Greville					i,301	i,306	i,317
F.C.[87]							
1. To Mr. John Milton	viii,69						
Sir B.G.							
1. An Elegy					iii,167		
Mr. H———							
1. Ode to Sleep					i,115	i,129	i,136
2. Ode on Beauty					—,120	—,134	—,141
3. Ode to Taste					—,124	—,138	—,145
4. Ode to Lady ——— on the Death of her Son					—,133	—,147	—,155
W.H.							
1. The Two Sneerers	xi,16						
T.M. Esq.							
1. Ode to Amanda	xi,12						
Rev. Mr. P.							
1. Epistle to a Lady	iv,97						
2. On the Death of a Lady	—,100						
3. Verses written before marriage	vii,97						
4. Verses written eight years after	—,98						
5. L'Amoroso	—,100						
H.P.							
1. Ode on Ranelagh	v,93						
P.P———s							
1. The Minister of State	ix,100						

87. Chalmers, vii,344, quotes the conjecture of H.J. Todd, editor of Milton's *Poetical Works*, 1801, that "F.C." might be Francis Cradock, a member of the Rota Club.

	F63	M67	M70	P68	P70	P75	P83
Mr. P——y							
1. The Sentiments of Truth	ix,113						
Mrs. P——y							
1. On the Nuptials of Lord Grey and Lady H. Bentinck	ix,116						
2. A Nuptial-Card	—,117						
E.R.							
1. Prologue	xii,81						
2. Pompilia	—,83						
3. Dialogue at Croydon	—,84						
4. Apology for running away	—,86						
5. Song to a tune in the Parting Lovers	—,87						
6. Song ["Tell me"]	—,88						
7. To Nannette	—,89						
8. To a Lady, on her obtaining a Prize in the Lottery	—,90						
9. Written at Venlo	—,91						
10. Epitaph on an Infant	—,91						
11. Inscription for the Statue of Edward VI	—,92						
12. The Death of Otho	—,92						
13. On a late Parricide	—,93						
14. The Roman Charity	—,93						
15. Epigram ["Cassandra"]	—,94						
16. Another ["Old Ayres"]	—,94						
17. Epitaph on a man who died at church	—,95						
18. On one who died of the Hyp	—,95						
19. Epigram on the false report of Mrs. H——y's Death	—,96						
20. Epitaph intended for my own tombstone	—,96						
C.S.							
1. Antipater's epigram on Water-mills	ii,71						
2. Lucian's epigram on a Column	—,72						
J.T.							
1. On the Physical Cause of the King's Death	iv,80						

	F63	M67	M70	P68	P70	P75	P83
J.E.W.							
1. The Rival Beauties	v,98						
2. Woman's Age	—,103						
3. The Breach of the Rivers	—,105						
4. On the great Fog in London 1762	vi,57						
5. On the Death of a Favourite Horse	—,60						
6. The Needle	ix,65						
7. Fire, Water and Reputation	—,88						
P.W.							
1. Prologue to the Distressed Mother	xi,119						
"A Lady"[88]							
A1. Song for the Park	iv,118						
A2. Verses on Lord Orrery	—,120						
B1. Moonlight Ode[89]	vii,68						
B2. Evadne to Emma	—,71						
B3. Hymn to Resignation	—,74						
B4. Imitation of Pastor Fido	—,76						
B5. Imitation of Metastasio	—,77						
B6. Sonnets from the Italian: From Petrarch	—,78						
B7. ———: From the same	—,79						
B8. ———: Sonnet of Faustina Maratti Zappi	—,80						
"_____"[90]							
1. Love Verses: To Damon	v,65						
2. ———: Elegy II	—,67						
3. The Recantation	—,73	177	143		iv,266	iv,300	iv,306
4. Love Elegies: Elegy I	—,76				—,251	—,285	—,291
5. ———: Elegy II	—,81				—,255	—,289	—,295
6. Inscription in Ham Walks	—,87				—,261	—,295	—,301
7. Verses written on a Pedestal	—,89	180			—,263	—,297	—,303

88. These ten pieces, though by unnamed "Ladies", form two sets of poems "by the same" and are therefore listed together as "unidentified" rather than distributed among the anonymous single items.

89. See note 88. The obituary notice of Mrs. Susanna Duncombe, wife of John Duncombe and daughter of Joseph Highmore, in *GM*, lxxxii, Pt.2, p.497 (1812) states that she "wrote a few poems for the *Poetical* Calendar", but does not identify them. As the poems "By a Lady" in F63, vol.vii, follow immediately on those of John Duncombe, it seems possible that these are Mrs. Duncombe's contributions.

90. Though the author's name is a blank, these pieces form a set and are therefore listed together as "unidentified" rather than distributed among the anonymous single items. Nos.4, 5, 6 and 7 were published in a volume of *Love Elegies and other Poems*, 1761 (reviewed in *CR*, July, xii,56), and nos.1, 2, 3 in *Love Verses*, also 1761, which is described in *CR*, November, xii,401, as "the second agreeable nosegay . . . lately culled" by the poet. As "The Recantation" (no.3) is listed in P75 and P83 as "by the same" as the "Love Elegies" (nos.4-7), it appears that both these volumes were by the same author.

Section C. Anonymous single poems

	F63	M67	M70	P68	P70	P75	P83
A1. Advice to a Lady	xi,107						
A2. Advice to an Author	v,123						
A3. Alexis[91]					iii,269		
A4. Anacreon Ode I	vi,62						
A5. Anacreon Ode XXVIII	ii,73						
A6. Anacreontic on the Spring	iv,12						
A7. Answer from Canterbury[92]	vii,51						
A8. August, an Ode	viii,1						
A9. Autumn	ix,13						
B1. Balaam						iii,256	iii,258
B2. Barreaux's Sonnet translated[93]	viii,65						
B3. Beldames, The					iv,156	iv,140	iv,142
C1. Comparison, The	vii,123						
C2. Contemplation	vi,7						
C3. Contraste to an Ode to Wisdom	iv,91						
D1. December	xii,1						
D2. Description of Spring in London	v,30						
E1. Elegy ["Tis Fate"]	vi,68						
E2. Elegy on a Humming-Bird					iv,144		
E3. Elegy on the Death of a Daughter	iv,73						
E4. Elm and the Vine, The		129					
E5. Epigram wrote on a Glass[94]	viii,19						
E6. Epigram on Bishop Atterbury's Funeral	viii,79						
E7. Epigram on Mrs. Collier	xi,97						
E8. Epigram on the Children of Israel	vi,67						
E9. Epilogue to the Englishman at Bourdeaux[95]		132	107				
E10. Epistle of M. de Voltaire[96]	xii,46	202	158				

91. "By a Lady"; from R. Lloyd's *St. James's Magazine*, February 1763.
92. Answer "by a Friend" to J. Duncombe's "Epistle from York" (q.v.).
93. Different from Robertson 3.
94. "By a Lady".
95. See note on the Prologue, Anon P4.
96. Translator not identified. Published, French and English, by Dodsley, 1755, 4°.

	F63	M67	M70	P68	P70	P75	P83
E11. Epistle from Mary the Cook[97]							
E12. Epitaph on General Wolfe	viii,122						
E13. Epitaph written in a Fit of the Vapours	xi,97						
E14. Excursion, The					iii,262		
F1. Fall of the Leaf, The	x,3						
F2. Farewell to Summer[98]	x,7						
F3. Folly of Atheism, The	v,122						
F4. Further Advice to an Author	vi,121						
G1. Genius of Britain, The[99]	vi,102						
H1. Harvest Scene	vii,6						
H2. Hermite's Addresse, The					iv,185	iv,171	iv,175
H3. Hope	xi,93	195					
H4. Horace, Ode IV, Book I, imitated	ii,8						
H5. Hospitable Oake, The[100]					iv,182	iv,168	iv,172
H6. Hours of Love, The: Night	vi,90						
H7. ———: Morning	—,92						
H8. ———: Noon	—,95						
H9. ———: Evening	—,99						
I1. In Imitation of Marloe	ii,59				iii,295		
I2. Inscription for General Wolfe's Monument	vi,115						
J1. July, an Ode	vii,1						
J2. June, an Ode	vi,1						
L1. Labour in Vain	v,110						
L2. Ladies' Lamentation, The	xi,91						
L3. Lady and the Linnet, The	vi,15	184					
L4. Liberty (from Meta-stasio)		140	255				
L5. Love Elegy ["The dewy morn"]	ii,113						
L6. Love Elegy (written at Oxford)[101]	v,119						

97. Signed "Mary Darby", presumably a pseudonym. See Anon R3 for the Answer.
98. By "Juvenis" of Gracechurch Street (*GM*, October 1761).
99. Different from the "Iambic Ode" of the same title by J.G. Cooper (q.v.).
100. *Nugae Antiquae*, ed. H. Harington, 1769,93. Ruth Hughey, *John Harington of Stepney*, Ohio, 1971, lists this among the doubtful poems of Harington.
101. Printed in the *London Chronicle*, 7 April 1763, with the signature "H.P.".

	F63	M67	M70	P68	P70	P75	P83
M1. Man of Kent, The	vii,111						
M2. Materials for a Monody	v,111						
M3. Modern Virtue			259	iib,72	ii,72	ii,72	ii,72
M4. Mulberry Garden, The	viii,5						
M5. "My Mind to me"[102]		148	119				
N1. November, an Ode	xi,1						
N2. November [Pastoral Elegy]	xi,3						
O1. October, an Ode	x,1						
O2. Ode ["The charms"]					iii,282		
O3. Ode on Lord Granby	iii,101						
O4. Ode on the Birth of Miss E.W.	viii,59						
O5. Ode to Horror[103]					iv,269		
O6. Ode to January	i,1						
O7. Ode to May	v,27						
O8. Ode to Morning[104]					iv,61	ii,299	
O9. Ode to Sensibility	xi,95	196					
O10. On Admiral Byng	vi,74						
O11. On Amoret's Recovery	iii,116						
O12. On Bentley's Emendations	viii,70						
O13. On Captain Forrester's travelling in the Highlands	i,10						
O14. On Laura's Grave					iii,288		
O15. On Mother Griffiths	iv,123						
O16. On my Hairs falling	ix,10						
O17. On seeing a Rose in October	x,13						
O18. On some dull, ill-natured verses	xi,102						
O19. On the Birth-day of Stephen Poyntz	ii,120						
O20. On the Death of a Young Gentleman	vi,71						
O21. On the Death of Dr. Morgan	ix,98						
O22. On the Death of Dr. Parne	x,14						

102. *Reliques*, i,312.
103. Published in *The Student*, 1751, ii,313, signed "Chimaericus Oxoniensis", Christ-Church, April 11, 1751; reprinted in *The Oxford Sausage*, 1764, 61, edited by Thomas Warton. W.L. Bowles in his edition of Pope, 1806, ii,362, said "The author was Thomas Warton"; but modern scholars are more cautious of attributing this parody of Collins to Warton (e.g. R. Lonsdale, *The Poems of Gray, Collins and Goldsmith*, 1969, 411).
104. Printed in *The World*, no.126, 29 May, 1755, with the signature "C.B.".

	F63	M67	M70	P68	P70	P75	P83
O23. On the Death of Miss W.	viii,62						
O24. On the First of February	ii,7						
O25. On the Marriage of Tame and Isis	iii,115						
O26. On the old Bust of Mr. Dryden	ii,119						
O27. On viewing an extensive Prospect from Aston Hills[105]	vii,5						
P1. Petrarch and Laura	xi,109	198	154				
P2. Present to a Young Lady with a Pair of Stockings[106]	x,45	167	136				
P3. Prologue to The Englishman at Bourdeaux[107]		131	106				
R1. Reflection on seeing the Picture of Belisarius[108]	x,64						
R2. Reflections on a Watch	ix,12						
R3. Richard the Farmer's Answer[109]	xi,100						
R4. Rookery, The		306	210				
S1. Sacred Lyric on a Thunder Storm	i,76						
S2. Salt Water[110]	x,121						
S3. Salt Water celebrated	xi,103						
S4. September, an Ode	ix,1						
S5. Shepherdess's Lamentation	xi,65						
S6. Song ["Unjustly, Cloe"]	xi,83						
S7. Song written by a Lady		117	98				
S8. Sonnet ["Ah, why did Heaven"]	xi,110						
S9. Spring, addressed to Myra	ii,5						

105. "By a Young Lady".
106. "By ——, Fellow of ——, Cambridge". Printed in Thomas Warton's *Oxford Sausage*, 1764, with the title "The New Year's Gift. Presented with a Pair of Silk Stockings, to Miss Bell Cooke, of Eton."
107. This comedy, by Favart, had no prologue or epilogue in its original edition. These were supplied by the English translator, "A Gentleman of Cambridge", with his translation, published by Wilkie, 1763.
108. Printed in *The Student*, 1751, ii,119, with the signature "F".
109. See Anon E11, "Epistle from Mary the Cook".
110. "By a Gentleman of the Navy."

	F63	M67	M70	P68	P70	P75	P83
S10. Stanzas on the Spring	iv,9						
S11. Studley Park[111]					iii,231		
S12. Suburban Preachment	ix,121						
S13. Supplication by a Lady	i,95						
S14. Supplication [another]	—,96						
S15. Sweet-William	v,117						
T1. Thought at Waking	xi,122						
T2. Thought in a Garden	vii,96						
T3. Thoughts on Lotteries	xi,105						
T4. To a Lady, with a Book entitled Visions	i,94						
T5. To a Lady, on her Birth-day	iv,7						
T6. To a Lover[112]					iv,184	iv,170	iv,174
T7. To Fame	xii,31						
T8. To Myrtilis[113]					iii,255	iii,249	iii,251
T9. To Sylvia	i,93						
T10. To the Rev. Mr. Fitzgerald	ix,61						
V1. Verses on the Arrival of Queen Charlotte					iv,273		
V2. Verses on the Death of Mrs. Oldfield	ii,116						
V3. Verses sent with a fine Carnation	vi,6						
V4. Verses written in London on the Approach of Spring				ii,143	ii,139	ii,153	ii,153
V5. Violet, The	iii,13						
W1. Winifreda[114]		153					
W2. Wish, The		217					
Y1. York and Kent	xi,107						
Z1. Zelis to Ibrahim	xi,87						

111. Different from Langhorne's poem of the same title.

112. *Nugae Antiquae*, ed. H. Harington, 1769, 130; signed "J.H. MSS. 1564", but not considered attributable to John Harington by Ruth Hughey, *The Arundel Harington Manuscript of Tudor Poetry*, Ohio, 1960.

113. Published in Anna Williams' *Miscellanies*, 1766, to which Johnson and his friends contributed. Attributed to Johnson himself in Bell's *Classical Arrangement of Fugitive Poetry*, 1789, vi,53, and Park's edition of Johnson's *Poetical Works*, 1811; but rejected by Nichol Smith, p.465. Not identified by Hazen, Johnson's *Prefaces and Dedications*.

114. Printed in Dodsley's *Collection*, iv,282 (1755), under the title "Song"; hence the footnote of apology by the editor of M67 for including it here. First printed by D. Lewis, *Miscellaneous Poems*, 1726, as "A Translation from the Ancient British"; reprinted by Percy, *Reliques*, i,346, with the title "Winifreda". See Courtney on erroneous attribution (copied by Chapman) to John Gilbert Cooper, whose "Father's Advice" (q.v.) was, according to Chalmers, "in imitation of the old song of Winifreda".

An old trite proverb let me quote	Garrick 1
And must thou leave us, Nancy,	"E.R." 5
And wilt thou, Romeo, still maintain	"Mr. H." 2
Aquarius rules the frozen skies	Cunningham, P. 1
Arise, divine Urania, with new strains	Smart 7
Arise, my Lycas; in yon woody wilds	Warton, T. 8
Arise, my soul! on wings seraphic rise	Blacklock 1
Around the world when Homer's genius shone	Anon Y1
As a young bird, as yet unus'd to fly	Murphy 1
As Cupid, the slyest young wanton alive	Fawkes 3
As Damon Chloe's painted form survey'd	Tickell 14
As late o'er Britain's chalky coasts	Cooper, J.G. 2
As near Porto-bello lying	Glover 1
As o'er the ocean's swelling tide	Wharton 1
As o'er the varied meads I stray	Anon A6
As once, if not with light regard,	Collins 8
As the plodding ploughman goes	Cunningham, J. 5
As, when diffus'd in solemn trance,	Scott, James 10
Assist, Urania, the adventurous song	Edwards, S. 1
At Dryden's tomb, inscrib'd with Sh———d's name	Anon O26
At large beneath this floating foliage laid	Thompson 3
At length, in pity to a nation's prayer	Harte 1
At length, poor suffering wretch, thy pangs are o'er	Anon O22
At length the gallant navy from afar	Spence 1
At length th'imperious lord of war	Whitehead, W. 1
At once to raise our reverence and delight	Lowth 2
At the close of the day, when the hamlet is still	Beattie 4
Author of being, source of light,	Wesley 1
Awake, my fair, the morning springs	Barclay 2
Away; let nought to love displeasing	Anon W1
Be dumb, be dumb, ye inharmonious sounds,	Thornton 1
Be gone, delusions vain,	Scott, James 11
Be still, my fears, suggest no false alarms	Hurd 1
Behold, my fair, where'er we rove	Johnson 3
Behold! The green fields yellowing into corny gold	Anon H1
Behold yon new-born infant, griev'd	Merrick 1
Beneath an awful gloom, a night of shade,	Thompson 21
Beneath this rural cell	Marriott 4
Beneath this stone the world's just wonder lies	Pitt 14
Beneath yon chain of barren rocks	Shepherd 5
Beneath yon flowery turf, the fairest head	Anon O14
Beneath yon snubby oak's extended shade	Mendez 6
Best of painters, show thy art	Anon A5
Blush, Wilmot, blush; a female muse	Pitt 9
Boast not your state, slaves of despotic sway,	Scott, John 14
Bright God of day, whose genial power	Fawkes 7
Bright goddess, I obey! with rapture hear	Keate 1
Brimful of anger, not of love,	Villiers 1
Bring hither, friend, O hither bring	Thompson 18

Bring me, O bring me to my Juliet's arms	Jones 1
Britons! rouse to deeds of death	Whitehead, W. 4
Britons, what unaton'd offence	Anon O10
By his hall chimney, where in rusty grate	Jenyns 1
By Love too long depriv'd of rest	"____" 3
By the lyre of Apollo, the locks of the Muses	Mendez 2
By the side of the stream that strays thro' the grove	Henley 2
By yon hills, with morning spread,	Thompson 4
Can this be he! could Charles, the good, the great,	Tickell 7
Cassandra from her spark receiv'd	"E.R." 15
Castalian goddess, come; nor slight the call	Emily 2
Cease, fair Aurelia, cease to mourn	Swan 1
Charming Annetta, but that I'm forbid	Denis 9
Child of the summer, charming rose,	Hervey 2
Close thine eyes, and sleep secure	Charles I 1
Come, fair Dorinda, and while beauty glows	Sheills 1
Come, gentle power, from whom arose	Scott, James 4
Come live with me and be my dear	Anon I1
Come live with me, and be my love	Marlowe 1
Come! lovely queen of endless smiles	Hawkesworth 4
Come, Melancholy! silent power	Carter 1
Come, rosy Health, celestial maid	Browne, I.H. 2
Come, shepherds, we'll follow the hearse	Cunningham, J. 2
Come, thou laughter-loving power,	Hartis 1
Commanding beauty, smooth'd by chearful grace	Walpole 6
Common births, like common things,	Whitehead, W. 2
Consum'd in trifles, thus the golden day	Fawkes 12
Contemplation, lovely fair,	Anon C2
Content! who oft art wont to dwell	Cockfield 1
Courtier, or swain! whom chance, perhaps, may bring	Cockfield 6
Dan Petrarch of old, it has often been said	Anon P1
Dan Pope first in vogue	Wooddeson 1
Dark was the night and dreary was the cell	Anon O23
Dark was the sky with many a cloud	"____" 6
Daughter of Chaos and old Night	Lloyd 2
Daughter of Exercise! at whose command	Woty 10
Daughter of God, Religion, lend thine aid	"Rev. Mr. P." 2
Daughters of Jove, prime source of sacred song	Cooper, T. 1
Dear Gem, I'll help you to a hint	Anon F4
Dear social bird, that oft with fearless love	Mulso 1
Dear Sir, — to all my trifles you attend	Pitt 2
Death, by a conduct strange and new	"E.R." 18
Death is a common fortune, sure to all	"J.E.W." 5
Deem not, ye plaintive crew, that suffer wrong	Melmoth 1
Deep in a grove, by cypress shaded	Cooper, J.G. 3
Deep silence reign'd, and dewy night	Cunningham, P. 2
Deform'd in dust, now Turnus press'd the ground	Mendez 1
Delightful Eden! parent stream	Langhorne 3

Delightful sovereign of the cheerful smile!	Woty 6
Destin'd, while living, to sustain	Wright 7
Detested deed! what rites shall purge the land	"E.R." 13
Distant to southern climes the sloping sun	Anon N1
Do thou, fair Liberty, descend	Schomberg 1
Down by the brook that glides thro' yonder vale	Dobson 1
Dreams, commonly we see,	Duncombe, J. 14
Duty demands, the parent's voice	Moore, E. 2
Early the sun his radiant axle guides	Anon V4
E'er yet, ingenuous youth, thy steps retire	Mason 6
Eliza, sweeter than the rose	Jeffreys 1
Endued with all that could adorn	Mills 2
Ere Saturn's sons were yet disgrac'd	Melmoth 2
Ere this can drown the tenderest husband's eyes	"S.B." 1
Ere this short winter's day be done	Canning 2
Ere yet I sing the round-revolving year	Mendez 2
Erst in Arcadia's londe much prais'd was found	Anon H5
Escap'd a race whose vanity ne'er rais'd	Walpole 4
Etherial daughter of the lusty Spring	Thompson 1
Evening now, from purple wings	Johnson 5
Exhausted by her painful throes	Ekins 1
Expatiate long in nice debate	Shepherd 3
Fair crystal fount, whose peaceful bed	"E.R." 2
Fair daughter once of Windsor's woods!	Tickell 5
Fair mirror of foul times, whose fragile sheen	Pope 6
Fair morn ascends; soft zephyr's wing	Mallett 2
Fairest daughter of the year	Whateley 4
Fallen are thy locks! for woeful winter hoar	Fawkes 6
Fame heard with pleasure — straight replied	Hardwicke 1
Far from her hallow'd grot, where mildly bright	Mason 7
Far in the windings of a vale	Mallett 5
Farewell, for clearer ken design'd	Collins 15
Farewell that liberty our fathers gave	Hammond 1
Farewell the pleasant violet-scented shade	Scott, John 3
Farewell the pomp of Flora! vivid scene	Anon S4
Farewell thou dimpled cherub joy	Warton, J. 5
Fast by the vale that bosoms Sennaa's pride	Irwin 3
Father of all! whose seat of rest	Merrick 5
Fatigued with illness, sick with pain	"A Lady" B3
Fervid now the sunbeam glows	Cunningham, J. 4
Fervid on the glittering flood	Cunningham, J. 4
Few and easy in your stay	Anon O16
Flavia the least and slightest toy	Atterbury 1
Florella, veil those radiant eyes	Robertson 2
Flowrets — wreaths — thy banks along	Anon M2
Fond man, retire to this lone cell	Cockfield 5
For daring feats of rustic sport	Pearson 1
For once, ye critics, let this sportive muse	Woty 17

For quiet, on Newmarket's plain   Duncombe, J. 4
Forgive, ye Nereids, if I song no more Diaper 1
Frail glass, thou bear'st my name as well as I Anon E5
Friend to my life, and parent of my youth Anon O19
Friend to the gloomy shade of night! "Mr. H." 1
Friend to the wretch, whom every friend forsakes Porteus 1
Friendship, adieu! thou dear, deceitful good Boyse 2
Friendship, how sweet! how comely dost thou seem Portal 3
From busy scenes, with peace alone retir'd Thompson 11
From earth's low prospects and deceitful aims Boyse 1
From frozen climes and endless tracts of snow Philips, A. 1
From gay St. James's Myra was returned "J.E.W." 1
From mountains of eternal snow Fawkes 15
From orchards of ample extent Cunningham, J. 8
From rosy fingers morning shook the dew Hawkesworth 7
From the fair gardens of the blooming East Barford 1
From the moss-grown coral cave Duncombe, J. 3
From these dread walls, this melancholy tow'r Keate 2
From these lone shades, and ever-gloomy bowers Pattison 2
From this tall promontory's brow Pitt 7
From your lyre-enchanted towers Smart 4
Full many a tedious hour, with care opprest Scott, James 2

Get along, sir — I hate you, that's flat "E.R." 3
Gladly the call of friendship I obey "Mrs. P———y" 2
Go, blessed tints, to Delia go Scott, James 5
God Alexander, it was said, Denis 2
God of my health, whose tender care Merrick 4
Good friend, forbear — the world will say 'tis spite Scott, James 1
Great, as from Porus' conquest, Philip's son Duncombe, J. 10
Great father of the skies, whose boundless sway Bowden 1
Great God! thy judgments are supremely right Anon B2
Grown old, and grown stupid, you just think me fit King 1

Hail, ancient book, most venerable code Tickell 17
Hail, blooming daughter of the youthful year! Anon V5
Hail, bright-eyed harbinger of sacred light! Portal 1
Hail! eldest of the monthly train Smart 2
Hail! empress of the star-bespangled sky! Woty 11
Hail, gentle summer, to this isle Fawkes 9
Hail! goddess of the silver star Woty 16
Hail, hallow'd Fane! amid whose mould'ring shrines Heber 1
Hail, happy Beldames! those your joys Anon B3
Hail, happy garden, happy groves, Thompson 9
Hail, noble Critic! whose pervading mind "A Lady" A2
Hail, pensive virgin, ever hail! Cockfield 2
(Hail, silent matron, ever hail!) Cockfield 2
Hail, Phillis, brighter than a morning sky Leapor 1
Hail, Queen of thought sublime! propitious power Ogilvie 1
Hail, sober nymph, in cloudy vest bedight! Henley 6

How rare the piece, where heaven and nature join   Wright 6
How sleep the brave, who sink to rest   Collins 9
How soon with nimble wings our pleasures haste   Marriott 9
How sweet the calm of this sequester'd shore   Carter 4
How sweet to recall the dear moments of joy   Parsons 2
How swift, alas! the rolling years   Cork 1
How venerable Turner's silver hairs!   Kennet 1
How weak the Atheist's argument, how odd!   Anon F3
How wondrous are thy works, O God most high   Anon O27
Hulse shook his head — poor Damon lay a-dying   Denis 5
Hush! let me search before I speak aloud   Foote 1
Hymen, (neglected god) this day appears   "Mrs. P———y" 1

I am, cry'd Apollo, when Daphne he woo'd   Tickell 8
I at my window sit and see   Anon A9
I'll sing you a ballad — O, that it were merry   Brereton 1
I whom thou see'st begirt with towering oaks   "C.S." 2
If all the world and love were young   Raleigh 1
If beauty's fairest form and each bright charm   Smith 1
If Greece with so much mirth did entertain   Locke 1
If happy spirits are allow'd to know   Wright 3
If he who first the apple sung, the fruit   Thompson 20
If Love and Reason ne'er agree   Hawkesworth 11
If, 'mid their round of pleasure, to convey   Duncombe, J. 8
If mortal hands thy peace destroy   Merrick 3
If ought of oaten stop, or pastoral song   Collins 13
If slighted Iris can your pity move   Henley 3
If 'tis not love, what passion rules my heart?   "A Lady" B7
If you can leave for books the crowded court   Pitt 6
If you, dear sir, will deign to pass a day   Fawkes 14
Imperial dome of Edward wise and brave   Warton, T. 5
In a fair summer's radiant morn   Walpole 5
In Aesop's days, when trees could speak   Anon E4
In angry mood, Jove once, they say,   Denis 3
In Anna's wars immortal Churchill rose   Anon C1
In antient days, as jovial Horace sings,   Smart 1
In antient days, when Arthur reign'd   Mickle 2
In aunciente days, tradition shows   Harington, H. 3
In Britain's isle, no matter where,   Gray 2
In Burton's favourite groves, alas, how chang'd   "Sir B.G." 1
In courts licentious, and a shameless age   Tickell 1
In fair Circassia, where, to love inclin'd   Collins 4
In gayer hours, when high my fancy ran   Savage 2
In Georgia's land, where Tefflis' tow'rs are seen   Collins 3
In Indian realms, ye critics say   Pearson 6
In my dark cell, low prostrate on the ground   Pattison 1
In prose I've wrote you many a journal   Fawkes 11
In pursuit of some lambs from my flock that had strayed   Anon L1
In silent horror o'er the boundless waste   Collins 2
In soft Narcissa's form united shine   Duncombe, J. 22

Madam, to you since fortune proves so kind	"E.R." 8
Mankind may rove, unvex'd by strife	Fawkes 5
Mark, mortals! mark with awe profound	Parsons 1
Matthew, whose skilful hand and well-worn spade	Edwards, T. 10
Meek Power! whose balmy-pinion'd gale	Ogilvie 5
Memory, be still! why throng upon the thought	Beattie 2
Methought I saw before my feet	Lyttelton 2
'Midst flowery meads and Avon's winding floods	Graves 3
Mindless of fate, in these low vile abodes	Pope 5
Mistaken fair one, check thy fancy's flight	Walpole 2
Mother and daughter! sister! friend and wife!	Pearson 9
Mourn, hapless Caledonia, mourn	Smollett 1
Much had I heard of fair Francelia's fame	Tickell 9
My gracious God, whose kind conducting hand	Edwards, T. 9
My minde to me a kingdom is	Anon M5
My pipe sounds a cheerfuller note	Anon H3
My system, doctor, is my own	Cheyne 1
My temples with clusters of grapes I'll entwine	Woty 15
Narcissa! still thro' ev'ry varying name	Carter 7
Nature! thy genial call I hear	Powys 1
Nature, with liberal hand, dispenses	Jago 1
Nice to the touch, as ermine chaste	"J.E.W." 7
Night, brooding o'er her mute domain	Blacklock 3
No fabled knight, in days of yore	Duncombe, J. 19
No longer hope, fond youth, to hide thy pain	"———" 1
No longer seek the needless aid	Duncombe, W. 2
No more fond Love shall wound my breast	Brooke 3
No more the morn with tepid rays	Hawkesworth 1
No more thus brooding o'er yon heap	Johnson 7
No Muses I implore their aid to bring	Belsham 1
No second love shall e'er my heart surprise	Hammond 12
Nor Phoebus, nor his tuneful choir	Anon S11
Not the soft sighs of vernal gales	Johnson 4
Not wrapt in smoky London's sulphurous clouds	West 2
Now Cynthia shone serene with silver light	Anon H6
Now Delia breathes in woods the fragrant air	Hammond 7
Now Evening had ting'd the gay landskip with gold	Ogilvie 7
Now from the southern climes returning spring	Anon S10
Now fye upon't, quoth Flattery	Fletcher 1
Now genial spring o'er lawn and grove	Whateley 3
Now ice-forming winter is melting away	Anon H4
Now new-vampt silks the mercer's window shows	Anon D2
Now Phoebus vertically shoots his rays	Anon H8
Now see my goddess, earthly born	Anon C3
Now summer, daughter of the sun	Warton, J. 7
Now the bright morning star, day's harbinger	Milton 1
Now the storm begins to lower	Gray 3
Nymph! that flies the crowded street	Cockfield 3
O Bean! whose fond connubial days	Gerrard 2

O born to bless some youth unknown	"Rev. Mr. P." 1
O could my Muse, with gentle Gay	Portal 4
O crown'd with honor, blest with length of days	Mallett 4
O far remov'd from my retreat	Brooke 2
O Goddess of the gloomy scene	Anon O5
O Goddess, on whose steps attend	Warton, J. 1
O Heberden, whose salutary care	Edwards, T. 5
O Johnson, fam'd for elegance and sense	Penny 2
O! may you walk, as years advance	Pinnell 4
O Night, dark Night! wrapt round with Stygian gloom	Whitehead, W. 3
O Nymph, whose powerful charms his heart could gain	"A Lady" B8
O Phoebus! down the western sky	Hawkesworth 17
O quickly leave thy lowly bed	Pearson 8
O sir, no more! I'll hear no more!	Pearson 7
O skill'd thy every reader's breast to warm	Thompson 7
O! sure the greedy wretch is pent	Anon S2
O take, O keep me, ever blest domain	Anon E10
O thou, by nature taught	Collins 7
O thou, ordain'd at length by pitying fate	Anon G1
O thou that glad'st my lonesome hours	Richardson 1
O thou, that to the moon-light vale	Warton, J. 6
O thou, the friend of man assign'd	Collins 5
O thou! the wonder of the present age	"F.C." 1
O thou, who bad'st the turtles bear	Collins 14
O thou who dwel'st upon the bough	Anon B4
O thou who 'mid the world-involving gloom	Ogilvie 3
O thou, who sit'st a smiling bride	Collins 10
O thou, whom Love and Fancy lead	Langhorne 6
O under various sacred names ador'd	West 1
O Venus! joy of men and gods	Broxholm 1
O whether with laborious clowns	Warton, J. 2
O'er Caledonia's ruder Alps	Anon O13
O'er curious models as you rove	Pitt 8
O'er midnight glass, or by the fair	Shepherd 2
O'er moorlands and mountains, rude, barren and bare	Cunningham, J. 9
O'er nature's soft bosom, by verdure unbound	Cunningham, J. 1
O'er the heath the heifer strays	Cunningham, J. 5
Of adverse fortune gentle Shenstone 'plained	Scott, John 10
Of damask cheeks and radiant eyes	Robertson 1
Of Eastern Virtue and Religion's force	Irwin 1
Of happiness terrestrial, and the source	Gay 1
Of trumpets, drums, guns, and the bold bloody battle	Anon A4
Of wasteful havock and destructive fate	Philips, J. 1
Offspring of folly and of pride	Smart 3
Oft have the chiefs, that deck the letter'd age	Duncombe, J. 21
Oft I've implored the gods in vain	Greville, Mrs. 1
Oh form'd alike to serve us and to please	Hammond 15
Oh! form'd by nature and refin'd by art	Tickell 16
Oh, may the worthy wight be blest	Anon S3
Oh, thou delight and sovereign of my soul	Anon Z1

Stript to the naked soul, escap'd from clay	Pope 1
Struck with religious awe, and solemn dread	Moore, A. 1
Sweet are the banks, when spring perfumes	Woty 13
Sweet as the fragrant breath of genial May	Cooper, J.G. 1
Sweet bird! that kindly perching near	Shaw 2
Sweet companion of the Muse!	Cotton 1
Sweet god of ease, whose opiate breath	Ogilvie 4
"Sweet is the love that comes with willingness"	Edwards, T. 8
Sweet Linnet, who from off the laurel spray	Edwards, T. 4
Sweet Muse of Hagley, whose melodious lyre	Langhorne 9
Sweet poplar shade, whose trembling leaves among	Potter 1
Take, holy earth, all that my soul holds dear	Mason 4
Tears, which the bar-rang'd orators command	Stevenson, W. 1
Tell me from whom, fat-headed Scot,	Wynter 1
Tell me where the weakness lies	"E.R." 6
Tender softness! infant mild!	Wright 1
Thanks, Nicè, to thy treacherous art	Anon L4
Thanks to thee, Nymph, whose powerful hand	Anon O9
That every female's a coquette	Stevenson, J.H. 2
That man is a vapour the Scriptures declare	Anon E13
That morning too shall dawn, when I shall rise	Anon T1
That Power Supreme that taught me first to breathe	"E.R." 20
The actual soul, by which man lives and moves	Duncombe, W. 3
The anxious struggle happily o'erpast	Anon E9
The balmy zephyrs o'er the woodland stray	Mickle 1
The Bard whose scenes this night your thoughts engage	Keate 6
The blissful scenes, which Virgil's pencil drew	Thompson 15
The bosom of earth is all matted with leaves	Woty 18
The broad sun, verging on the close of day	Panting 3
The charms which blooming beauty shows	Anon O2
The curfew tolls the hour of closing gates	Duncombe, J. 2
The deeds of discord, or in prose or rhyme,	Harris 1
The dewy morn her saffron mantle spreads	Anon L5
The diamond's and the ruby's blaze	Fordyce 1
The feather'd game that haunt the hoary plains	Fitzgerald 1
The festive roar of laughter, the warm glow	Emily 1
The fragrant painting of our flowery fields	Tickell 13
The garden blooms with vegetable gold	Anon A8
The gentle maid, whose hapless tale	Walpole 7
The god, in whose gay train appear	Mallett 3
The goldfinch swells his little throat	Marriott 2
The graces and the wandering loves	Hughes 1
The grave, great teacher, to a level brings	Walpole 1
The greatest swain that treads th'Arcadian grove	Tickell 12
The greedy merchant ploughs the sea for gain	Somervile 1
The Latian dame, a prison's nightly guest	"E.R." 14
The Lesbian lute no more can charm	Brooke 1
The little brook that erst my cot did lave	Mendez 8
The lofty beeches, and their sacred shade	Potter 2

The Lord is my shepherd, my guardian and guide   Byrom 1
The man, who sharpen'd first the warlike steel   Hammond 11
The midnight clock has toll'd; and hark, the bell   Mason 1
The Muses were on Pindus met   Lockman 1
The naked grove now shivers at the blast   Anon O1
The night is come, like to the day   Browne, Sir T. 1
The north-east wind did briskly blow   Grainger 1
The old Egyptians hid their wit   Chesterfield 1
The opening East now streaks a ruddy ray   Panting 1
The opera first Italian masters taught   Tickell 2
The peaceful evening breathes her balmy store   Mickle 4
The prince of all the feather'd kind   Ramsay 1
The race of critics, till of late, were grac'd   Anon O15
The radiant ruler of the year   Akenside 1
The rivers once their union broke   "J.E.W." 3
The sable queen of shades retires   Hudson 1
The shape alone let others praise   Akenside 3
The shrinking brooks and russet meads complain'd   Hawkesworth 2
The slightest of favours bestow'd by the fair   Dodd 4
The solemn hand of sable-suited night   Anon L6
The sons of man, by various passions led   Mendez 3
The sprightly messenger of day   Anon O8
The stars obscur'd from view retire   Anon O4
The sun comes up apace, and thro' the signs   Anon J1
The sun, diffusing genial fires   Woodhouse 1
The sun far southward bends his annual way   Scott, John 4
The swain who own'd yon rural cot   Cockfield 9
The tree of deepest root is found   Thrale 1
The virgin, when soften'd by May   Cunningham, J. 6
The wealthy Cit, grown old in trade   Lloyd 1
The weary look, desponding air   Marriott 10
The world's a bubble, and the life of man   Bacon, F. 1
Their antient friends, as now they nearer drew   Tickell 15
There fled the fair, that all beholders charm'd   Hoole 1
There was a time when from those hapless schools   Wodhull 1
These, the last lines my trembling hands can write   Gerrard 3
Think not I mean thy tenderness to move   Pearson 4
This bubbling stream not uninstructive flows   Graves 2
This day, which saw my Delia's beauty rise   Hammond 10
This morn, when at the inn I'd sold my hay   Anon R3
Tho' Britain's Genius hung his drooping head   Duncombe, J. 20
Tho' gold and silk their charms unite   Johnson 8
Tho' in Judaea's mead the verdant blade   Cockfield 11
Tho' the seasons must alter, ah! yet let me find   Brerewood 3
Tho' thy decrees, great God, are wise   Robertson 3
Thou! at whose touch the snow-clad mountains smoke   Hawkesworth 10
Thou child of nature, Genius strong   Lloyd 4
Thou restless fluctuating deep   Carter 5
Thou silent power, whose welcome sway   Akenside 6
Thou that at deep dead of night   Warton, J. 8
Thou to whom the world unknown   Collins 6

Thou tranquil daughter of the day	Woty 14
Thou, who art thirsty for a poet's name	Anon A2
Thou, who survey'st these walls with curious eye	Johnson 9
Thou, whom long since I number'd for my own	"———" 2
Though kindly silent thus my friend remains	Scott, John 6
Thousands would seek the lasting peace of death	Hammond 6
Three hours from noon the passing shadow shows	Scott, John 2
Thrice happy flower, what heavenly aid	Anon O17
Thrice happy who free from ambition and pride	Browne, I.H. 1
Thrice has the spring beheld thy faded fame	Akenside 4
Thrice has the year its varied circuit run	Scott, John 11
Thro' grief to death men oft have stole	"J.T." 1
Thro' groves sequester'd, dark and still	Hawkesworth 16
Throw an apple up a hill	Cowley 1
Thus Death, the king of terrors, spoke	Pinnell 2
Thus on the banks of Seine	Atterbury 4
Thus where the Seine thro' realms of slavery strays	Atterbury 4
Thus, when bleak winds their baleful influence shed	Anon O11
Thy friends have access to a nobler part	Langhorne 8
Thy justice, heavenly King! and that great day	Glynn 1
Thy park, Kimbolton, and surrounding shade	Hutchinson 2
Thy size, bright taper, does so quickly waste	Pinnell 3
Thy spirit, Independence, let me share	Smollett 2
Time flies, Nannette, to seal our doom	"E.R." 7
Time was when poets play'd the thorough game	Whitehead, W. 5
'Tis done! unclouded sets the radiant year	Duncombe, J. 9
'Tis fate commands — reluctant I depart	Anon E1
'Tis night, dead night, and o'er the plain	"———" 4
'Tis now the dreary hour of night	Woty 1
'Tis said, dear sir, no poets please the town	Pitt 4
To Albion's bards the Muse of History spoke	Scott, John 13
To Amaryllis, lovely nymph, I speed	Fawkes 2
To chant in rugged verse, hoarse muse arise	Harington, H. 2
To chase the timorous hare young Dian knew	Bacon, P. 1
To fair Fidele's grassy tomb	Collins 18
To lift the low, the proud depress	Anon L3
To please the fair, what different ways	Anon P2
To scenes where Taste and Genius dwell	Cockfield 13
To speed the sad moments away	"S.B." 4
To thee, my fair, this beauteous flower I send	Anon V3
To woo green April, lo the sun	Woty 7
To you, Eliza, be these lays consign'd	Whateley 2
Tonight, ye Britons, let the deathless name	Duncombe, J. 7
Too long, by some fatality misled	Anon P3
Too long has love engross'd Britannia's stage	Tickell 3
Too much my heart of beauty's power hath known	Akenside 5
Tremble, thou Earth! th'anointed poet said	Smart 8
True wit is like the precious stone	Anon O18
Turn, gentle hermit of the dale,	Goldsmith 1
'Twas at the silent, solemn hour	Mallett 1

'Twas from a sloe-tree's leafless spray	Pearson 3
'Twas on the border of a stream	Langhorne 5
'Twas when the slow-declining ray	Ogilvie 6
Two youths of noble birth, whose wayward fate	Irwin 5
Unequal, how shall I the search begin	Madan 1
Unfold the gates of ever-flowing time	Anon O6
"Ungrateful Rome!" — the generous Scipio said	"P. P———s" 1
Unjustly, Cloe, you suggest	Anon S6
Uprose the King of Men with speed	Gray 4
Vanae sit arti, sit studio modus	Lowth 1
Vengeance, arise from thy infernal bed	Brown 1
Venus, most histories agree,	Keate 5
Virtue and Fame, the other day	Lyttelton 1
Virtue, stern tutress, hail!	Shepherd 1
— Virtuous youth!	Anstey 1
We came to Harburg late at night	Duncombe, J. 12
Wear pleasure, Stella, on thy face	Wright 4
Welcome, Philanthes, to thy native fields	Warton, T. 11
Welcome, sweet May! far thro' a world of snow	Anon O7
Welcome, sweete Death, the kindest friend I have	Essex 3
Welcome thou sober evening, calm and gray	Portal 2
Welcome to light! advent'rous pair!	Dalton 1
Well may they, Wentworth, call thee young	Garrick 2
What a change has befallen my grove!	Pearson 2
What are the falling rills, the pendent shades	Pope 3
What do scholars, and bards, and astronomers wise	Chesterfield 2
What does the sad presaging mean?	Marriott 8
What friendship gives, sweet girl, approve	"S.B." 2
"What is Nobility?" you wish to know	Dalton 2
What kings henceforth shall reign, what states be free	Tickell 6
What means, honest shepherd, this cloud on thy brow?	Anon N2
What means this awful sight? why round me shine	Onely 1
What pious whims, my fair, are these?	Anon A1
What pleasing form commands the lifted eye	Thompson 12
What scenes of bliss my raptur'd fancy fram'd	Hammond 14
What! shall the causeless curse of fools controul	Hawkesworth 14
What spacious veins enrich the British soil	Yalden 1
What tho' nor glittering turret rise	Brown 2
What! tho' thou com'st in sable mantle clad	Woty 19
What tho' your art my hopes evade	"S.B." 3
What tranquil road, unvex'd by strife	Fawkes 4
What wonders brave Hawke and Boscawen have done	Duncombe, J. 24
Whate'er you think, good sirs, in this agree	Garrick 3
When a Nymph at her toilet has spent the whole day	Hawkesworth 13
When approach'd by the fair dewy fingers of spring	Brerewood 1
When Brunswick first appear'd, each honest heart	Tickell 4
When Cain and Abel their first offerings made	Anon E7

When Egypt's king God's chosen tribes pursued	Anon E8
When Envy saw your Gothic structure rise	Mendez, Jael 1
When evening gales allay the summer's heat	Duncombe, J. 15
When every tongue great George's praise recites	Penny 1
When fierce Bellona doubtful held the scale	"E.R." 12
When first the kingdom to thy virtues due	Warton, T. 4
When greatness claims, or merit gives	Anon V2
When here, Lucinda, first we came	Dorset 1
When in full pride autumnal fields appear	Anon M4
When, in your language, I unskill'd address	Milton 3
When Jove at first from nothing call'd out all	Hawkesworth 5
When Milton's forfeit life was in debate	Anon O12
When Moab's wiles had failed to move	Anon B1
When Music, heavenly maid, was young	Collins 16
When now the spring had burst, with genial power	Duncombe, J. 17
When our first Father, thro' the dreary waste	Percy 1
When our great Lord at Emmaus appear'd	Wharton 2
When Pallas saw the piece her pupils wrought	Pitt 10
When rough Helvetia's hardy sons obey	Langhorne 2
When sable midnight on the fields and woods	Warton, T. 10
When sleep's all-soothing hand with fetters soft	Denton 1
When snows descend, and robe the fields	Hervey 1
When stately structures Lowther grace	Dalton 4
When Stella strikes the tuneful string	Johnson 10
When the nymphs were contending for beauty and fame	Anon S7
When the trees are all bare, not a leaf to be seen	Brerewood 4
When Venus saw Adonis dead	Fawkes 8
When wit and science trim'd their wither'd bays	Cawthorne 2
When, young, life's journey I began	"———" 5
Whence come these dismal sounds that fill our ears?	Stone 1
Whence comes my love, O heart disclose	Harington, J. 1
Whence this unwonted transport in my breast?	Akenside 7
Whene'er superior force defies	"E.R." 4
Where are those hours, on rosy pinions borne	Carter 6
Where art thou, Fancy, visionary maid?	Hudson 2
Where bold and graceful soars, secure of fame	Tickell 18
Where free from sense, intrench'd in earth no more	Anon O21
Where mouldering piles conceal the sculptor's hand	Irwin 2
Where's now Othello's hair-breadth 'scapes	Anon O3
Where shall the Muse, that on the sacred shell	Warton, T. 6
Where sighs the zephyr to yon lonely tree	Jerningham 2
Where Thames with pride beholds Augusta's charms	Savage 1
Where the fair streams of fam'd Euphrates stray	Cockfield 10
Where the light cannot pierce, in a grove of tall trees	Brerewood 2
Whether Stella's eyes are found	Johnson 6
Which way, Calistan, whither dost thou lead	Warton, T. 12
While born to bring the Muse's happier days	Collins 17
While calm you sit beneath your secret shade	Hammond 4
While George, in sorrow, bows his laurell'd head	Anon E12
While I was fond, and you were kind	Atterbury 2

While I with fond officious care	Warton, J. 4
While in the bosom of this deep recess	Warton, T. 9
While Learning's pleasing cares my friend detain	Scott, John 7
While, lost to all his former mirth	Collins 12
While night in solemn shade invests the pole	Carter 8
While other bards in venturous song proclaim	Duncombe, J. 5
While others sing of high imperial states	"J.E.W." 6
While rosy wreaths the goblet deck	Dodington 2
While sickness rends this tenement of clay	Wright 5
While silent streams the moss-grown turrets lave	Marriott 12
While superstition teaches to revere	Walpole 3
While thro' irriguous meads pleas'd Isis stray'd	Anon O25
While wisdom shines with light divine	Henley 1
While yet no amorous youths around thee bow	Melmoth 3
While you enjoy a calm and cool retreat	Anon T10
While you, fair Anna, innocently gay	Percy 2
While you 'mid spring's gay months deplore	"Mr. H." 4
Who but remembers yesterday	Dorset 2
Who is this thilke old Bard which wonneth here?	Thompson 8
Who reads Lost Paradise, the fall	Duncombe, W. 4
Who shall awake the Spartan fife	Collins 11
Whoe'er thou art, whom chance or choice may bring	Cockfield 6
Whose is this image? Academic Glory	Hardinge 1
Why are our thoughts on lords alone intent?	Anon M1
Why asks my friend what chears the passing day	Scott, John 9
Why, Celia, is your spreading waist	Moore, E. 1
Why didst thou rase such woeful wayle	Anon T6
Why droops the head, why languishes the eye?	Pinnell 1
Why, gentle god, this long delay	Scott, James 6
Wide o'er the world misfortune bears her sway	"P.W." 1
Wish'd morn is come — a cheerful ray of light	Anon H7
With each perfection dawning on her mind	Jerningham 1
With malice fell	Stevenson, J.H. 6
With Muckworm lately as I sat	Barclay 4
With no poetic ardour fir'd	Pope 4
"With prudence choose a wife" — Be thy first care	Edwards, T. 7
With restless agitations tost	Carter 2
With rolling time that all things change	Barclay 3
With song, sweet babe, we celebrate thy birth	Anon S15
With wine, more wine, deceive thy master's care	Hammond 5
With wonted candor once again peruse	Duncombe, J. 6
With wreath of yellow crocus bound	Woty 3
Within a lonely gallery's awful gloom	"A Lady" B1
Without preamble, to my friend	"Countess of C" 1
Woman's age is seldom known	"J.E.W." 2
Would Chloe know the highest bliss	Pinnell 5
Ye baleful followers of the Blatant Beast	Mendez 4
Ye curious hands, that hid from vulgar eyes	Collins 20
Ye dazzling lamps, ye jocund fires	"H.P." 1

Ye fair, for whom the hands of Hymen weave	Jerningham 3
Ye female artizans, who grind the corn	"C.S." 1
Ye foplings, and prigs, and ye wou'd-be smart things	"A Lady" A1
Ye generous Britons, sons of fair renown	"Mr. P———y" 1
"Ye green-hair'd Nymphs, whom Pan allows"	"———" 7
Ye groves, with venerable moss array'd	Marriott 1
Ye holy cares that haunt these lonely cells	Langhorne 4
Ye maids of the village attend	Anon S5
Ye northern blasts, and Eurus, wont to sweep	Glover 2
Ye patriot crowds, who burn for England's fame	Johnson 1
Ye Persian maids, attend your poet's lays	Collins 1
Ye sacred spirits! while your friends distress'd	Pitt 13
Ye scenes, that engag'd my gay youth	Gerrard 4
Ye shepherds so careless and gay	Lloyd 7
Ye sordid wretches! chain'd to rules	Woty 4
Yes — every hopeful son of rhyme	Anon V1
Yes, it is past; the fatal stroke is given	Marriott 11
Yes, to the sages be it told	Greville, F. 2
Yes, yes, my friend, my heart I own	Dodsley 2
Yet do I live! O how shall I sustain	Shaw 1
Yet once more, glorious god of day	Fawkes 10
Yet once more, sweetest queen of song	Scott, James 3
Yet once more, ye lov'd poplars, and once more	Potter 3
You ask me, madam, if the Muse	Dalton 3
You ask why in that garland fair	Berenger 1
You rejoice without hope, and you hope without reason	"A Lady" B5
Your kind itinerary letter	Ellis 1
"Your servant, sir," says surly Quin	"W.H." 1

BARCLAY, James (b.1747)
Son of the Rev. James Barclay, a Scottish schoolmaster, who ran an Academy at Tottenham. Educated at Balliol College, Oxford, 1764-68 (B.A.). No separate publication of his poems (P70) is known. Isaac Reed says he died young. (P83; *Al.Oxon.*; *History of the Robinhood Society*, 1764,126)

BARFORD, Richard (b.1722)
One of the fifteen children of the Rev. William Barford, of Wilton, Wilts. Educated at Hart Hall, Oxford, 1740-43 (B.A.). Took orders and became D.D., 1761. Published *A Poem on Knolls-Hill*, 1745; *The Great Shepherd*, 1757 (P75); *Virtue, an Ethic Epistle*, 1758. (*Al.Oxon.*; Hoare, *Dunworth*, 125,205; *Downton*, 11; *MR*, xix,590; *CR*, iii,381)

BELSHAM, James (d.1770)
Dissenting minister of Bedford. His two sons, Thomas and James, both figure as writers in *DNB*. But his only known separate publications were two Odes in Latin Alcaics. (H.G. Tibbutt, "The Belshams of Bedford", *Bedfordshire Magazine*, v,no.34,1955; *DNB*, for his sons)

BRERETON, Charlotte (b.1720)
Youngest daughter of Thomas Brereton of Chester and Jane Hughes of Mold, Flintshire, who both published poetry. From 1736, when she was sixteen, to 1742 she contributed verses to *GM* under the pseudonym "Carolina" (like her mother, "Melissa"). Her song, "The Rattle" (F63), is dated 1732, which means she wrote it about the age of twelve (*Poems* by Mrs. Jane Brereton, 1744, preface; Foxon, Brereton, Jane and Thomas; *GM*, 1735-1742)

CANNING, George (1736?-1771)
Father of the statesman; eldest son of Stratford Canning of Garvagh, Londonderry. Came to London in 1757 to study law; called to the Bar, 1764. Published a modernised version of *Horace's First Satire*, 1762; the *Epistle from William Lord Russell*, 1763 (P70); a translation of Cardinal Polignac's *Anti-Lucretius*, 1766; *Poems*, 1767. In 1768 he married Mary Ann Costello, a beauty with no fortune, to whom he wrote his *Birthday Offering* (P70), and was thereupon disinherited. The difficulties of supporting a growing family, daughter and son (George, the future Premier), wore him out and he died on his son's first birthday, 11 April 1771. (P83; *DNB*, for the son; *Mid.Temple*; *MR*, 1770,406)

COCKFIELD, Joseph
A Quaker, of Upton, West Ham, he was a close friend of the Quaker poet, John Scott of Amwell, who addressed an *Ode* to him. He contributed moral and religious articles to the *Christian Magazine* and a few short poems found a place in various miscellanies. Though his letters to the Rev. Weeden Butler (1765-71) show him preparing a number of literary and botanical projects, Nichols says he does not appear to have published anything with his name. (Nichols, *Illust.*, v,753-808; John Scott, *Poems*, 1782,198; I.A. Gordon, *Shenstone's Miscellany*, 1952,159)

DALRYMPLE, Hew (d.1774)

Scottish advocate; father of the celebrated courtesan, Grace Elliott. Published *Woodstock Park, an Elegy*, 1761 (P68); and *Rodondo, or the State Jugglers* (a pro-Scottish satire) in three parts, 1763-70. Died as Attorney-General of Grenada, 1774 — the year that Grace left her husband for her first lover. (*DNB*, Elliott, Grace; Mrs. Elliott, *Journal of my Life*, 1859; *N&Q*, 1st Ser.,ix,589)

DENIS, Charles (1705?-1772)

Son of a Huguenot refugee; elder brother of Admiral Sir Peter Denis. Studied surgery in Paris, but gave up his practice for a literary life in London. Accompanied Garrick to Paris in 1751. Published *Select Fables*, 1754; contributed fables to Robert Lloyd's *St. James's Magazine*, 1762-3, and to F63; collaborated with Lloyd in translating the *Moral Tales of M. Marmontel*, 2 vols, 1764; and translated de Belloy's tragedy *The Siege of Calais* (never acted despite his friendship with Garrick). (*DNB*, for his brother; Little & Kahrl, letters 107,300,354; *Biog.Dram.*, i,182; *NFH*, v,18; Edward Thompson, *Nauticks*, 1783, i.90)

DIAPER, William (1685-1717)

See Dorothy Broughton, ed. *The Complete Works of William Diaper*, 1951.

DOBSON, John

Captain in the merchant navy. His pastoral, *Robin* (F63), was printed in 1746 in *GM*, where he was described as "commander of the Prince Rupert snow, in the Barbary trade". (*GM*, xvi,609)

EDWARDS, Samuel (b.1702)

Scholar of Westminster School and Trinity College, Cambridge (M.A., 1729). His poem, *The Copernican System* (F63), was published by the Cambridge University Press, 1728. (*Al.Cantab.*; *Old Westminsters*; Foxon E19)

EMILY, Charles (1734-1762)

Eldest son of Edward Emily of West Clandon, Surrey. Scholar of Westminster School and Trinity College, Cambridge, of which he became a Fellow in 1759. Succeeded to the family estates in 1760, but died, unmarried, 1762. Published *The Praises of Isis* (P70), a friendly tribute to the rival university, 1755. His poem, *Death* (F63; P68) was printed posthumously in Lloyd's *St. James's Magazine*, October 1762. (P83; *Old Westminsters*; *Al.Cantab.*; Manning & Bray, i,140,143)

FITZGERALD, Gerald (1740-1819)

Professor successively of Laws (1783) and Hebrew (1790) at Trinity College, Dublin, where he had been educated. Published *The Academick Sportsman*, Dublin, 1773 (P75); *The Injured Islanders* [of Tahiti], 1779; and collected *Poems*, 1797. (*Al.Dublin.*)

FLETCHER, Philip (1706-1765)

See Courtney, 32. Besides his poems in Dodsley and F63, there are a few more in Nichols' *Select Collection*, vol.vi. But no collection of his verses is known. (*Al.Oxon.*; *GM*, 1,123)

GERRARD, John

Curate of Withycombe-in-the-Moor, Devon, when he published his *Poems*, 1769, which included the four reprinted in P70. Though his preface says he was young and his volume was well received by the reviewers, no other poems by him are known. (*MR*, xlii,185)

GREVILLE, Fulke (1717?-1806?)
GREVILLE, (Mrs) Frances (1728?-1789)
Husband and wife, in high society, often mentioned by Horace Walpole and Fanny Burney, of whom Mrs. Greville was the godmother. One of Walpole's *Beauties*, "very witty and very pretty", she is believed to have collaborated in her husband's *Maxims, Characters and Reflections*, 1756, which included the two poems reprinted in F63, P68, etc. Her universally popular *Prayer for Indifference* (F63, M67, P68, etc.) was said to have been provoked by her husband's difficult temper. (Lewis, *Berry*, 47n; *Deffand*, i,124n; *Mann*, i,126n; C. Lloyd, *Fanny Burney*, 1936, *passim*; A.R. Ellis, *Early Diary of Fanny Burney*, 1913, 2 vols, *passim*; Burke's *Peerage*, 1970, art. Warwick; Hoare, *Ambresbury*, 103)

HAYES, Daniel (1736-1767)
Born at Limerick, son of a landowner and lawyer. Entered Trinity College, Dublin, 1751, and moved to the Middle Temple, London, 1756. Here his riotous behaviour gained him the nickname of "Buck Hayes". Published an *Epistle to Charles Churchill*, 1761; *The Authors*, a satire, 1766; *An Epistle from the Abbé de Rance*, 1766. Died in 1767, aged thirty-one, and his *Works in Verse*, with his Life, were published posthumously in London, 1769. They do not include the *Elegy* printed in P75, which describes his unhappy life in London and his nostalgia for Limerick. (P83; *Al.Dublin.*; *Mid. Temple*; Hayes, *Works in Verse*, 1769, preface)

HEBER, Reginald (1729?-1804)
Rector of Malpas, Cheshire, and former Fellow of Brasenose College, Oxford. Father of Richard, the book-collector, and Reginald, Bishop of Calcutta. His *Elegy written among the Tombs of Westminster Abbey* (P75) was published in 1762. (*Al.Oxon.*; *DNB*, for the sons)

HUDSON, Thomas (1709-1784)
Schoolmaster, appointed Headmaster of Hexham Grammar School, Northumberland, 1742, with a local curacy. Quarrelled with both the school governors and his parishioners and was removed in 1748. Ended as curate of Blanchland, Co. Durham, from 1753 until his death. His publications included an *Ode on the Death of Frederick Prince of Wales*, 1751; *Poems on Several Occasions*, Newcastle-on-Tyne, 1752; *Four Odes*, 1759 (F63, P68, etc.); *Ode for Her Majesty's Birthday*, 1765. (P83; *History of Northumberland*, iii,224, iv,28, vi,338; *MR*, xxi,85)

HUTCHINSON, Benjamin (1733-1804)
Born at Durham, where he was ordained priest, 1759. Appointed Vicar of Kimbolton, Hunts, 1761. Consulted by Percy on Northern and Scottish words in the ballads. Published *Kimbolton Park* (P70, etc.) and *Marriage, an Ode*, (P75, etc.), both in 1765 and in folio. (*Reliques*, i,xviii; Brooks, *Hailes*, 26n)

JONES, Lewis (b.1721?)
Vicar of Caldicut, Monmouthshire. Educated at Jesus College, Oxford, (B.A., 1744). The poem printed in F63 is taken from his collection *Alpha and Omega*, Gloucester, 1758. (*Al.Oxon.*)

MADAN, (Mrs) Judith (Cowper) (1702-1781)
See Courtney, 80-83.

MENDEZ, Jael (Mrs. Hampden PYE) (1736-82)
Daughter of Solomon Mendez, of Red Lion Square, Holborn, and probably related to
Moses Mendez. Though she figured as "Miss M———" in M67, she had by then been
married twice, her second husband being brother of Henry James Pye, later Poet
Laureate. Privately printed *Poems by a Lady*, 1767; reprinted in 1772 as *Poems by
Mrs. Hampden Pye*, including her poem in M67 and Walpole's reply. Garrick staged her
farce, *The Capricious Lady*, 1771, and despite its failure they remained friends,
conducting a lively correspondence while she was living in Paris between 1774 and
1778. (Lewis, *Cole*, i,367n; Little & Kahrl, iii,1116n; *L.Stage*, Pt.4,iii,1547)

MILLS, Andrew Hervey
In 1755 his ballad *Colin and Lucy* (F63) was published surreptitiously as a genuine
Elizabethan production. He therefore renamed it *Allen and Ella* (P68, etc.) when he
printed it in his volume of *Bagatelles*, 1767. (*NFH*, v,303)

MOORE, Anthony (b.1727)
Son of Thomas Moore, of Grampound, Cornwall. Entered Exeter College, Oxford,
1745, and published *A Poetical Representation of the Passion*, 1747. Took orders and
appointed Vicar of Stratton, Cornwall, where he produced *Verses on seeing the
Fossilry at Pendarves* (GM, 1755); *A Soliloquy in a Country Churchyard* (GM, 1758;
F63); *An Essay on the Art of Preaching*, Falmouth, 1758; *A Sea-Piece written on the
Coast near Mount's Bay in Cornwall*, 1760. For his authorship of the *Elegy written
among the Ruins of a Nobleman's Seat in Cornwall* (F63), see note in the Index of
Authors. (*Al.Oxon.*; Foxon P706; *Parochial History of Cornwall*, Truro, 1867, iv,190;
GM, Dec. 1755; March, 1758; *MR*, xix,585; xxiii,172)

ONELY, Richard (1723-1787)
Born at West Haddon, Northants, and educated at Christ's College, Cambridge. Took
orders, 1748, and was appointed Headmaster of Clipstone Grammar School, Northants.
In 1768 he moved to Kent as Rector of Speldhurst, in 1772 adding Ashurst, where he
died in 1787. Apart from a Latin version of Pope's *Messiah, The Charge of Cyrus the
Great* (P68) seems to have been his only poetical publication. (*Al.Cantab.*; *MR*,
xiv,520; xviii,271)

PANTING, Stephen (b.1733)
Born at Wotton-under-Edge, Glos, and educated at Balliol College, Oxford. B.A., 1754.
Took orders some time between 1761, when he published his *Four Elegies* (F63) and
1766, when he figures as the Rev. Mr. Panting in *The Union*, third edition, with the
same four poems. (*Al.Oxon.*; *The Union*, 1766, 105; *MR*, xxvi,152)

PEARSON, Thomas (1740-1782)
Born and educated at Burton, Westmoreland. Entered the service of the East India
Company in Bengal, 1760, and rose to the rank of Major. Several of his poems (P75,
etc.) are concerned with life in Calcutta. He returned to England in 1770, but unwisely
went back after six years to India, where he died in 1782. (P83)

PENNINGTON, Miss (1734-1759)
See Courtney, 59. Though her *Copper Farthing* (F63), an imitation of John Philips'

Splendid Shilling, was a popular anthology piece and earned her a place in John Duncombe's *Feminead* (1754), her Christian name is nowhere mentioned.

PENNY, (Mrs) Anne (1731-1784)

Daughter of a Welsh clergyman called Hughes, she married a naval officer called Christian and had one son, who became an Admiral. Her second husband was a Customs officer named Peter Penny. She published *Anningait and Ajutt, a Greenland Tale*, 1761, versified from the *Rambler* and dedicated to Dr. Johnson (F63); Gessner's *Pastorals*, 1762; *Poems with a Dramatic Entertainment*, 1771, with Johnson, Percy and the "Bluestockings" among the subscribers. Her husband died in 1779, leaving her in distress, and a second subscription was raised (this time including Horace Walpole) for her *Poems*, 1781, consisting largely of the same contents. (Nichols, *Illust.*, vi,185; vii,541; *Biog. Dram.*, i,566; *DNB*, for her son Sir Hugh Cloberry Christian)

PINNELL, Peter (1722-1783)

Son of Richard Pinnell, merchant, of Streatham, Surrey. Educated at Eton and Trinity College, Cambridge, he took orders in 1744 and enjoyed a prosperous ecclesiastical career. He does not appear to have published any of his poems (F63) separately. (*Al.Cantab.*; *Al.Oxon.*; *GM*, xviii,432)

POWYS, Thomas (1736-1809)

Second son of Philip Powys and Isabella Lybbe, who inherited Hardwick House, near Whitchurch, Oxon. His elder brother married the diarist, Mrs. Lybbe Powys, who described him as "a most gentle, able man, a great favourite in society, and has a remarkable talent for rhyming". Entered St. John's College, Oxford, 1753; took orders, 1761, and after multiple preferments became Dean of Canterbury, 1797. Published a poetical version of *The Tablet of Cebes*, 1759, while still at Oxford; but otherwise his verses (P70, etc.) are to be found only in collections of fugitive poetry. (*Al.Oxon.*; *Diaries of Mrs. Philip Lybbe Powys*, 1899, *passim*; Nichols, *Illust.*, vi,678; *NFH*, 18-26; Halkett & Laing, vi,2)

SWAN, John

M.D., of Newcastle-under-Lyme, Staffs. Best known for his translation of the *Works of Dr. Thomas Sydenham*, 1742, for which the young Samuel Johnson wrote the introductory Life. About 1740 he contributed several poems to *GM* under the pseudonym "Amasius", including the verses *To Miss Aurelia C———r*, mistakenly attributed to Collins in F63 and appended to Johnson's *Life of Collins*. (Hill, ii,130n; Courtney & Nichol Smith, *Bibliography of Johnson*, 1925, 12; *GM*, vols.ix,x,xi)

THOMAS, (Mrs) Elizabeth (1714-1779)

Sister of General Sir Jeffery (later Lord) Amherst and wife of the Rev. John Thomas, Rector of Notgrove, Glos. Hence the pseudonym "Cotswouldia" under which she wrote her poetical compliment to Shenstone (M67). (Williams, 589n; Collins' *Peerage*, 1812, viii,169)

VERNON, William (b.1735)

Born at Wolverhampton of poor parents, he received only a rudimentary education; yet he began writing verses from the age of sixteen. He was apprenticed to a buckle-maker, but soon enlisted as a private in the Buffs and in 1757, while in camp in the Isle of Wight, visited Winchester and met the Wartons, who encouraged him to publish by subscription his *Poems on Several Occasions*, 1758. His next poem, *The Parish Clerk*

(P75, etc.), attracted the notice of Dr. Johnson, who sent a copy to Shenstone. Verses by Vernon in *GM* included lines written in a copy of Young's *Night Thoughts* at Winchester College (Aug. 1759) and a verse epistle on the capture of Belleisle, in which Vernon took part (July 1762). With the peace he got his discharge from the army and, according to Isaac Reed, was given a post as corrector of the press in London, but died soon after. (The Rector of Hanbury, Worcs, cited by Brooks, was a different William Vernon). (P83; Williams, 516n; Brooks, *Shenstone*, 27; Boswell, *Life of Johnson*, ed. Hill/Powell, 1950, v,268n; *GM*, xxix,383; xxxii,33)

WHATELEY, Mary (Mrs. Darwall)
Born in Walsall of a well-known Staffordshire family. In 1761 she sent a collection of her poems to Shenstone, who encouraged her to publish; her *Original Poems* were brought out by subscription in 1764 (P70, etc.). Around 1770 she married the Rev. John Darwall, Vicar of Walsall, himself a writer of verses, and, judging by her poem on their fifteenth wedding day, enjoyed a happy and fruitful marriage. After his death in 1789 she published a second collection of *Poems on Several Occasions*, under her married name, 2 vols, Walsall, 1794. (Williams, 589; *MR*, xxx,445)

WOODDESON, Richard (1704-1774)
Son of the Rev. Richard Wooddeson, Vicar of Findon, Sussex, and father of the jurist of the same name. Educated at Magdalen College, Oxford, of which he was chaplain, 1725-28. Became a schoolmaster and from 1733 to 1772 was Headmaster of the Free School, Kingston-on-Thames, where his pupils included Gibbon, Hayley, Keate, Steevens, Wakefield and other writers. His own writings were confined to a Latin prosody, some sermons and a few fugitive poems (F63). (*DNB*, for the son; *GM*, 1823, i,181,225; Gibbon, *Autobiography*, World's Classics, 1935, 24; G. Wakefield, *Memoirs*, 1804, i,42-52)

WRIGHT, (Mrs) Mehetabel (Wesley) (1697-1751)
"Hetty" Wesley, daughter of the Rev. Samuel Wesley and sister of the Methodist leaders John and Charles, was born at her father's rectory at Epworth and by the age of eight was acting as his amanuensis. An unhappy love affair led to an unsuitable marriage with a dissipated plumber named Wright in 1725. Her husband's neglect and the deaths of her infants made her life full of suffering, reflected in her poems (F63), which were originally published in *GM* and the *Christian Magazine*. Others are to be found in the Lives of her brothers, but no separate collection was ever made. (*DNB*, father; G.J. Stevenson, *Memorials of the Wesley Family*, 1876, 298-320; *GM*, vi,155,348,740)

WYNTER, John
Born in Somerset, he studied medicine under Dr. John Freind. After various adventures, including a visit to Jamaica and two years in Reading Gaol, he settled in Bath. His controversial works on the hot baths led to a feud with Dr. George Cheyne and the exchange of epigrams with the "fat-headed Scot" (F63). Even after Cheyne's death in 1743 he continued the feud in his eccentric privately-printed medley, *Les Badinages de Monsieur Wynter, or Wynter's Whims*, 1744. (*Wynter's Whims*, passim; *DNB*, Cheyne, George)